A
CALL
to the
UNCONVERTED
to Turn and Live

Register This New Book

Benefits of Registering*

- ✓ FREE **replacements** of lost or damaged books
- ✓ FREE **audiobook** – *Pilgrim's Progress,* audiobook edition
- ✓ FREE information about new titles and other **freebies**

www.anekopress.com/new-book-registration

*See our website for requirements and limitations.

A
CALL
to the
UNCONVERTED
to Turn and Live

Directions *and* Persuasions
for a Sound Conversion

RICHARD BAXTER

We enjoy hearing from our readers. Please contact
us at www.anekopress.com/questions-comments
with any questions, comments, or suggestions.

Contents

The Great Success that Attended the Call When First Published

I t may be proper to begin with an account of this book given by Mr. Baxter in his own words that was found in his study after his death:

I published a short treatise on conversion entitled *A Call to the Unconverted*. The occasion of this was my conversation with Bishop Usher while I was at London. He had approved of my method and directions for *Peace of Conscience*,[1] and insisted that I write directions suited to the various conditions of Christians, and also against specific sins. I reverenced the man, but disregarded his recommendation, supposing I could do nothing better than what had already been done.

But after he was dead, his words went deeper to my mind, and I was determined to obey his counsel. However, in regard to the first type of people, the ungodly, I thought forceful persuasions were more appropriate than instructions only. Therefore, I published this little book, which God has blessed with unexpected success beyond all the rest that I have written, except for *The Saints' Everlasting Rest*. In a little more than a

---

1   This can be found in Volume 9 of *The Practical Works of Richard Baxter*, and is titled *The Right Method for a Settled Peace of Conscience and Spiritual Comfort, In Thirty-Two Directions*.

year, about twenty thousand copies of this book were printed by my own consent, and about ten thousand since, besides many thousands that have been printed without permission, which poor men stole in order to make money.

Through God's mercy, I have been told about almost entire households converted by this small book that I did not give much importance to. As if all this in England, Scotland, and Ireland were not mercy enough to me, God, since I was silenced, has sent it over in His message to many beyond the seas, for after John Eliot had printed the entire Bible in the Indian language, he next translated this book, my *Call to the Unconverted,* as he wrote to us here.

Yet God would make even more use of it, for Mr. Stoop, the pastor of the French Church in London, being driven out by the displeasure of his superiors, was pleased to translate it into French. I hope it will not be unprofitable there, nor in Germany, where it has also been printed.

It may be good to also mention Dr. Bates's account of the author and of this useful book. In his sermon at Mr. Baxter's funeral, he said the following:

His books of practical divinity have been used to bring about more conversions of sinners to God than any other books printed in our time. While the church remains on earth, these books will be of continual power to recover lost souls. There is a vigorous pulse in them that keeps the reader awake and attentive. His *Call to the Unconverted* – how small in size, but how powerful! Truth is spoken in it with such authority and power that it makes the reader lay his hand upon his heart and find that he has a soul and a conscience, even though he lived before as if he had none. He told some friends that six brothers were converted by reading this *Call,* and that every week he received letters of some who had been converted by his books. He spoke this with most humble thankfulness that God was pleased to use him as an instrument for the salvation of souls.

The Author's Preface

*To all unsanctified people who will read this book,
especially of my hearers in Kidderminster:*[2]

M en and Brethren,
    The eternal God, who made you for a life everlasting, and has redeemed you by His only Son, when you had lost it and yourselves, being concerned about you in your sin and misery, has given us the gospel, has sealed it by His Spirit, and has commanded His ministers to preach it to the world. With pardon being freely offered to you, and heaven being set before you, He calls you away from your fleshly pleasures, and away from following after this deceitful world, and desires to acquaint you with the life that you were created and redeemed for before you are dead and past remedy (2 Chronicles 36:16).

He does not send you prophets or apostles who receive their message by immediate revelation, but He calls you by His ordinary ministers, who are commissioned by Him to preach the same gospel that Christ and His apostles first delivered. The Lord sees how you forget Him and your latter end, and how you

---

2   Richard Baxter began his pastoral ministry in Kidderminster, England, where he remained for the next nineteen years.

give little consideration to everlasting things, as people who do not understand what they have to do or suffer.

He sees how bold you are in sin, how fearless you are of His threatenings, how careless you are of your souls, and how the works of unbelievers are in your lives – while the belief of Christians is in your mouths. He sees the dreadful day at hand, when your sorrows will begin and you must lament all this with unavailing cries in torment and desperation. The remembrance of your folly will then tear your hearts if true conversion does not prevent it now.

In compassion to your sinful, miserable souls, the Lord, who knows your situation better than you can know it, has made it our duty to speak to you in His name (2 Corinthians 5:19) and to tell you plainly of your sin and misery, what your end will be, and how sad a change you will soon see, even if you continue a little longer. Having bought you at such a precious cost as the blood of His Son Jesus Christ, and having made you such a free and general promise of pardon, grace, and everlasting glory, He commands us to offer all this to you as the gift of God, and to plead with you to consider the necessity and worth of what He offers.

> We believe and obey the voice of God, and we come to you with His message.

He sees you and has compassion on you, even while you are drowned in worldly cares and pleasures, eagerly following childish toys and wasting that short and precious time to pursue emptiness and vanity when you should be preparing for an everlasting life. Therefore, He has commanded us to pursue you and tell you how you will lose your labor and are about to lose your souls. He has commanded us to tell you also what greater and better things you could certainly have if you would listen to His call (Isaiah 55:1-3).

We believe and obey the voice of God, and we come to you

with His message. He has commanded us to preach – to be ready in season and out of season (2 Timothy 4:1-2) to lift up our voice like a trumpet and show you your transgressions and your sins (Isaiah 58:1).

Tragically, to the grief of our souls and to your ruin, you stop your ears, stiffen your necks, harden your hearts, and send us back to God with tears to tell Him that we have obeyed His commands and have delivered His message, but that it will do you no good, nor did you even take it seriously. Oh, that our eyes were as fountains of tears so that we might lament our ignorant, careless people who have Christ and pardon and life and heaven before them, but do not have hearts to know or value them (Jeremiah 9:1)! They could have Christ and grace and glory just as others do – if it were not for their willful negligence and contempt!

Oh, that the Lord would fill our hearts with more compassion to these wretched souls so that we might cast ourselves even at their feet, follow them to their houses, and speak to them with our bitter tears. We have preached to many of them for a long time in vain. We speak plainly to make them understand, but many of them will not understand us. We speak serious, piercing words to make them feel, but they will not feel.

If the greatest matters would work with them, we would wake them. If the sweetest things would work, we would persuade them and win their hearts. If the most alarming things would work, we would at least frighten them from their wickedness. If truth and sincerity would work with them, we would soon convince them. If the God who made them and the Christ who bought them would be heard, the case would soon be different with them. If Scripture would be heard, we would soon prevail. If reason, even the best and strongest reason, would be heard, we would undoubtedly quickly convince them. If they would listen to experience, even their own experience and the experience of all the world, the matter would be remedied. Yes, if they would listen to the conscience within them, the situation would be better with them than it is.

But if they will listen to nothing, if they refuse to hear anything, then what can we do for them? If the almighty God of heaven is ignored or disregarded, who, then, will they regard? If the immeasurable love and blood of a Redeemer is ignored, what, then, will they value? If heaven has no desirable glory with them, and everlasting joys are worth nothing to them; if they can joke about hell, laugh about the bottomless pit, and play with the consuming fire – and can do so when God and man warn them of it – what can we do for such souls as these?

Once more, in the name of the God of heaven, I will deliver to you the message that He has commanded us, and will leave it in these lines to convert you or condemn you, to change you or rise up in judgment against you, and to be a witness to your faces that you once had a serious call to turn from your ways and turn to God. Hear, all you who are workers of the world and servants of the flesh and Satan! Listen, you who spend your days in looking after prosperity on earth, and who drown your consciences in drinking, in gluttony, in idleness, and in foolish sports! You are aware of your sin, yet you will continue in sin, as if you set God at defiance and ask Him to do His best and not hold back!

Listen, all you who pay no attention to God, who have no heart for holy things, and who feel no delight in the Word or worship of the Lord, or in the thoughts or mention of eternal life. Hear, you who are careless of your immortal souls, and never give one hour in inquiring about your situation, whether you are sanctified or unsanctified, and whether you are ready to appear before the Lord! Listen, all you who, by sinning in light, have sinned yourselves into faithlessness and who do not believe the Word of God!

He who has an ear to hear, let him hear the gracious and yet fearful call of God! His eye is always upon you. Your sins are recorded, and you will surely hear of them again. God keeps the book now, and He will write it upon your consciences with His terror – and then you will also keep it yourselves!

Oh, sinners, if you only knew what you were doing, and whom you are offending all this time! The sun itself is darkness before the glory of that Majesty whom you daily abuse and carelessly provoke. The sinning angels were not able to stand before Him, but were cast down to be tormented with devils – and dare such worms as you so carelessly offend and set yourselves against your Maker?

Oh, that you even understood a little what a dreadful situation that wretched soul is in who has opposed the living God! The word of His mouth that made you can unmake you. The frown of His face will cut you off and cast you out into outer darkness. How eager the demons who have tempted you are to be dealing with you. They simply wait for the word from God to take and use you as their own – and then in a moment, you will be in hell.

If God is against you, all things are against you. For all who love this world, this world is only your prison. You are merely reserved in it to the day of wrath (Job 21:30). The Judge is coming, and your soul is going. Yet a little while, and your friend will say of you, "He is dead." Then you will see the things that you now despise, and you will feel that which now you will not believe. Death will bring such an argument that you cannot answer. It will be an argument that will powerfully discredit your arguments against the Word and ways of God.

Then your mind will quickly be changed. Then be an unbeliever if you can. Then stand by all your former words that you were inclined to utter against a holy and a heavenly life. Then make good that cause before the Lord that you were inclined to plead against those who taught the Bible, and against the people who feared God. Then stand by your old opinions and contemptuous thoughts of the diligence of the saints. Make ready now your strong reasons, and then stand up before the Judge and plead like a man for your fleshly, worldly, and ungodly life. However, know that you will be pleading with One who will not be intimidated by you, nor will be as easily evaded as your fellow creatures.

Oh, deceived, wretched soul! There is nothing but a slender veil of flesh between you and that amazing sight that will quickly silence you, change your tone, and make you of another mind! As soon as death has drawn this curtain, you will see that which will quickly leave you speechless. How quickly that day and hour will come! When you have had only a few more lighthearted hours, only a few more pleasant meals, and just a little more of the honors and riches of the world, your portion will be spent and your pleasures will be ended – and then all is gone that you had set your heart upon. Of all that you sold your Savior and salvation for, there is nothing left but the bitter reckoning – giving an account to God for your life. As a thief who sits happily in a tavern spending the money that he has stolen as men are quickly coming to apprehend him, so is it with you. While you are drowned in cares of fleshly pleasures and delighting in your own shame, death is coming quickly to seize you and to carry your soul to such a place and state that you now little know or think about.

Suppose when you are bold and active in your sin that a messenger were quickly coming to apprehend you and take away your life. Even if you did not see him, if you knew that he was coming, it would ruin your fun, for you would be thinking

> There is nothing but a slender veil of flesh between you and that amazing sight that will quickly change your tone.

of how soon he will arrive, and you would be listening for his knock at your door. Oh, that you could only see what haste Death makes, even though he has not yet overtaken you! There is no messenger as swift or certain. As sure as the sun will be with you in the morning, although it has many thousand and hundred thousand miles to go in the night, Death will be quickly and certainly with you.

Then where will your sport and pleasure be? Will you then joke and continue your opposition? Will you then mock those who warned you? Is it better then to be a believing saint, or a carnal person who delights in the things of this world? Then whose will all these things be that you have gathered (Luke 12:19-21)? Do you not observe that days and weeks are quickly gone, that nights and mornings come swiftly, and that they speedily follow each other?

You sleep, but your damnation does not slumber. You linger, but your judgment, to which you are reserved for punishment, lingers not (2 Peter 2:3-9). Oh, that you would be wise and understand this, and that you would consider your latter end (Deuteronomy 32:29)! He who has an ear to hear, let him hear the call of God in this day of his salvation.

Oh, careless sinners, I wish you only knew the love that you unthankfully neglect and the preciousness of the blood of Christ that you despise! Oh, that you only knew the riches of the gospel! Oh, that you only knew a little of the certainty, the glory, and the blessedness of that everlasting life that you will not now set your hearts upon or be persuaded to seek diligently now (Matthew 6:13; Hebrews 11:6; 12:28)!

If you only knew the endless life with God that you now neglect, you would quickly cast away your sin, change your mind and life, change your course and company, turn the direction of your devotion, and spend your energy and time another way. How resolutely you would despise giving in to those temptations that now deceive you and lead you astray! How zealously you would pursue that most blessed life for yourself! How earnest you would be with God in prayer! How diligent you would be in hearing, learning, and inquiring! How serious you would be in meditating on the laws of God (Psalm 1:2)! How fearful you would be of sinning in thought, word, or deed! How careful you would be to please God and grow in holiness!

Oh, what a changed person you would be! Why should not the sure Word of God, which opens to you these glorious and eternal things, be believed by you and prevail with you?

Yes, let me tell you that even here on earth, you do not much understand the difference between the life you refuse and the life you choose! The sanctified are conversing with God while you dare hardly think of Him, and when you are conversing with mere earth and flesh. Their conversation is in heaven, yet you are complete strangers to heaven. Your belly is your god, and you are occupied with earthly things (Philippians 3:18-20). They are seeking after the face of God, but you seek for nothing higher than this world. They are busily storing up treasure for an endless life where they will be equal with the angels (Luke 20:36), but you are preoccupied with a shadow and a fleeting thing of emptiness.

How low and cheap your earthly, fleshly, sinful life is in comparison with the noble spiritual life of true believers! I have often looked on such people with grief and pity as I saw them trudge about the world, wasting their lives and caring and laboring for nothing but a little food and raiment, a little fading money, fleshly pleasures, or empty honors – as if they had nothing higher with which to concern themselves.

What difference is there between the lives of these people and of the beasts that perish, that spend their time working, eating, and living only that they may live? They do not taste the inward heavenly pleasures that believers taste and live upon.

I would rather have a little of their comfort, which the anticipation of their heavenly inheritance provides them, even if I had all their scorn and suffering with it, than to have all your pleasures and deceitful prosperity.

I would not take one of your secret stings of conscience, and dark and dreadful thoughts of death and the life to come, for all that the world has ever done for you, or all that you can reasonably hope that it might do. If I were in your unconverted carnal state, and knew only what I know, and believed only what I now believe, I think my life would be a foretaste of hell. How often I would be thinking of the terrors of the Lord, and of the dreary day that is hastening on! Certain death and hell would still be waiting for me. I would think of them by day, and dream of them by night. I would lie down in fear, rise in fear, and live in fear, afraid that death would come before I were converted. I should have little happiness in anything that I possessed, little pleasure in any company, and little joy in anything in the world as long as I knew that I was under the curse and wrath of God. I would still be afraid of hearing that voice: *Thou fool, this night shall thy soul be required of thee* (Luke 12:20). That dreadful sentence would be written upon my conscience: *There is no peace, saith the* LORD, *unto the wicked* (Isaiah 48:22; 57:21).

Oh, poor sinners! You could live a more joyful life than this if you were only willing, truly willing, to listen to Christ and come home to God. You could then draw near to God with boldness, call Him your Father, and comfortably trust Him with your souls and bodies. If you look upon the promises, you could say, "They are all mine." If you look at the curse, you may say, "I am delivered from this." When you read the law, you could see what you are saved from. When you read the gospel, you could see Him who redeemed you. You could see the course of His love, His holy life, and His sufferings, and you could follow Him in His temptations, tears, and blood in the work of your salvation. You could see death conquered and heaven opened, and you could see your resurrection and glorification provided for in the resurrection and glorification of your Lord.

If you look on the redeemed, you could say, "They are my brethren and companions." If you look on the unredeemed, you could rejoice to think that you are saved from that state. If you look upon the heavens, the sun, the moon, and the innumerable stars, you could think and say, "My Father's face is infinitely more glorious. He has prepared higher matters for His saints. That is only the outward court of heaven. The blessedness that He has promised me is so much higher that flesh and blood cannot behold it."

If you think of the grave, you could remember that the glorified Spirit, the living Head, and the loving Father all have such a near relation to your dust in that grace that it cannot be forgotten or neglected, but will more certainly revive than the plants and flowers in the spring – because the soul is still alive, which is the root of the body; and Christ is alive, which is the root of both soul and body. Even death, which is the king of fears, could be remembered and entertained with joy as being the day of your deliverance from the remnant of sin and sorrow – the day that you believed and hoped and waited for, when you will see the blessed things that you had heard of, and will find by present joyful experience what it means to choose the better part (Luke 10:42) and to be a sincere, believing saint.

What do you say? Is it not a more delightful life to be assured of salvation and to be ready to die than to live as the ungodly, who have their hearts *overcharged with surfeiting and drunkenness, and the cares of this life, and so that day comes upon [them] unawares* (Luke 21:34)? Would you not live a comfortable life if you were made an heir of heaven, and if you were certain to be saved when you leave the world? Look around you, then, and consider what you do. Do not cast away such hopes as these for mere nothing. The flesh and the world can give you no such hopes or comforts.

I have just three requests to ask you, and I will be done.

1. I ask you to seriously read over this small book. You also have family members who need it, so I ask you to read it over and over to them. If those who fear God would occasionally go to their neighbors and give this or some other book to them on this subject, they might be a means of winning souls. If people will not be persuaded to take such a small amount of effort for their own salvation as to read such short instructions as these, they do not much regard themselves, and will most rightly perish.

2. After you have read over this book, I would urge you to go alone and think a little about what you have read, and consider, as in the sight of God, whether it is true, whether its message does not hit close to your soul, and whether it is not time to take these matters seriously in your own life.

I also request you to get upon your knees and seek the Lord, asking Him to open your eyes to understand the truth and to turn your hearts to the love of God. Beg Him for all that saving grace that you have so long neglected, and continue to do this every day until your hearts are changed. Even more, I ask you to go to your godly pastors (who are set over you to take care of the health and safety of your souls, just as physicians do for the health of your bodies) and desire them to direct you in what course to take, acquainting them with your spiritual condition so that you may have the benefit of their advice and ministerial help. If you do not have a faithful pastor at home, make use of some other godly person for this great need.

3. When, by reading, consideration, prayer, and ministerial advice, you are then acquainted with your sin and misery, with your duty and remedy, do not delay, but immediately forsake your sinful company and routine, and turn to God and obey His call. If you love your souls, take care that you do not continue in your ways against so loud a call of God, and against your own knowledge and conscience, lest it will go worse with you in the day of judgment than with Sodom and Gomorrah (Matthew 10:15). Inquire of God as a man who is willing to know the truth, and do not stubbornly cheat your soul.

Search the Holy Scriptures daily, and see whether these things are so (Acts 17:11). Examine impartially whether it is safer to trust heaven or earth, whether it is better to follow God or man, the Spirit or the flesh, whether it is better to live in holiness or sin, and whether an unsanctified state is safe for you to abide in one day longer. When you have found out which is best, decide accordingly, and make your choice without any more delay.

> If you love your souls, take care that you do not continue in your ways against so loud a call of God.

If you desire to be true to your own souls, and do not love everlasting torments, I urge you, as from the Lord, that you will simply take this reasonable advice. Then at your deathbed, how boldly might we comfort and encourage your departing souls! At your burial, how comfortably might we leave you in the grave in expectation of meeting your souls in heaven and of seeing your bodies raised to that glory!

However, if most of you will still continue in a careless, ignorant, carnal, worldly, or unholy life, and all our desires and labors cannot so much prevail as to keep you from knowingly condemning yourselves, we must then imitate our Lord, who delights Himself in those few who are jewels, and in a little flock that will receive the kingdom, when most people will reap the misery that they sowed.

In nature, excellent things are few. The world does not have many suns or moons. Only a little of the earth is gold or silver. Princes and nobles make up only a small part of the sons of men. There are not a great number of people who are learned, judicious, or wise here in this world. Therefore, since the gate is strait and the way is very narrow (Matthew 7:14), and there are only few who find salvation, God will still have His glory and pleasure in those few.

When Christ will come *with his mighty angels, in flaming fire taking vengeance on them that know not God, and that obey not the gospel of our Lord Jesus Christ*, His coming will be *glorified in his saints*, and admired in all true believers (2 Thessalonians 1:7-10).

And for the rest, as God the Father condescended to create them, and God the Son did not refuse to bear the penalty of their sins upon the cross and did not judge such sufferings vain (although He knew that by refusing the sanctification of the Holy Spirit they would finally destroy themselves), so we who are His ministers do not judge our labor completely lost, even though these people are not gathered (see Isaiah 49:5).

Reader, my part with you will be over once you have read this book, but sin is not yet done with you, even those sins that you thought had been forgotten long ago. Satan is not yet done with you, either, although he may now be out of sight. Nor is God done with you simply because you will not be persuaded to be finished with deadly reigning sin.

I have written you this work of persuasion as one who is going into another world where the things are seen that I mention here – and as one who knows that you must soon be there yourself. If you will ever meet me with comfort before the Lord who made us; if you will ever escape the everlasting plagues prepared for the final neglecters of salvation and for all who are not sanctified by the Holy Spirit and who do not love the communion of the saints as members of the holy universal church; and if you ever hope to see the face of Christ the Judge, and the majesty of the Father with peace and comfort, and to be received into glory when you are turned out of this world with nothing, then I plead with you, I instruct you, to hear and obey the call of God and to resolutely turn so that you may live.

However, if you will not, even when you have no true reason for it except that you will not, I summon you to answer it before the Lord, and I require you to bear witness there that I gave you warning, and that you were not condemned for lack of a call to turn and live – but because you would not believe it and obey it. This must also be the testimony of your sincere author,

Richard Baxter

December 11, 1657

Introduction

Say unto them, As I live, saith the Lord God, I have no pleasure in the death of the wicked; but that the wicked turn from his way and live: turn ye, turn ye from your evil ways; for why will ye die, O house of Israel? – Ezekiel 33:11

It has been the astonishing wonder of many people, including myself, to read in the Holy Scriptures how few will be saved, and to see that the greatest part even of those who are called will be everlastingly shut out of the kingdom of heaven and will be tormented with the demons in eternal fire. The unsaved do not believe this when they read it, and therefore they must feel it. Those who do believe it are forced to cry out with Paul, *O the depth of the riches both of the wisdom and knowledge of God! How unsearchable are his judgments, and his ways past finding out!* (Romans 11:33).

Nature itself teaches us all to lay the blame of evil works upon the doers, and therefore, when we see any awful thing done, a principle of justice provokes us to inquire after him who did it so that the evil of the work may return the evil of shame upon the person who did the evil act. If we saw a man killed and cut

1

in pieces along the road, we would immediately ask, "Oh! who did this cruel deed?" If the town was purposely set on fire, you would ask what wicked wretch did that.

In the same way, when we read that many souls will be miserable in hell forever, we must ask ourselves how this will happen, and whose fault it is. Who is so cruel as to be the cause of such a thing as this? We will meet with few who will confess their own guilt. It is indeed confessed by all that Satan is the cause, but that does not resolve the doubt because he is not the main cause. He does not force people to sin, but tempts them to sin, leaving it to their own wills whether they will do it or not. He does not carry people into a tavern, force open their mouths, and pour in the drink. He does not force them to stay there so that they cannot go to God's service, nor does he force their hearts not to think holy thoughts.

> Satan does not force people to sin, but tempts them to sin, leaving it to their own wills whether they will do it or not.

The choice, then, is between God Himself and the sinner. One of them must necessarily be the main cause of all this misery, whoever it is, for there is no one else to blame it on – and God denies that He is to blame. He will not take it upon Himself to be the cause of people's sin, and the wicked usually deny that they are to blame. They will not take it upon themselves, and this is the disagreement that is here guiding my text.

The Lord complains of the people, and the people think it is God's fault. The same controversy is discussed in Ezekiel 18. They plainly say that *the way of the LORD is not equal* (Ezekiel 18:25). So here they say, *If our transgressions and our sins be upon us, and we pine away in them, how should we then live?* (Ezekiel 33:10). It is as if they say, "If we must die and be miserable, how can we help it?" They speak as if it were not their fault, but God's.

However, God, in our text, clears Himself of it and tells them how they may help it if they want to. He persuades them to use the means, and if they will not be persuaded, He lets them know that it is their own fault. If this will not satisfy them, He will not refrain from punishing them. He will be the Judge, and He will judge them according to their ways. They are not His judges or their own judges, for they lack authority, wisdom, and impartiality. Their criticism of God and quarreling with God will not help them or save them from the execution of that justice at which they murmur.

The words of this verse, Ezekiel 33:11, contain: (1) God's clearing Himself from the blame of their destruction. He does not do this by rejecting His law that the wicked will die, nor by disallowing His judgment and execution according to that law or giving them any hope that the law will not be executed. Rather, He does this by professing that it is not their death that He takes pleasure in, but their returning so that they may live – and He confirms this to them by His oath. (2) A specific exhortation to the wicked to return, wherein God not only commands, but also persuades and condescends to reason the case with them, even asking them why they will die. The direct hope of this exhortation is that they may turn and live.

The secondary or reserved desire, upon supposition that the first is not attained, are these two: (1) To convince them by the means that He used that it is not God's fault if they are miserable. (2) To convince them from their plain disobedience and rebellion in rejecting all His commands and exhortations that it is their own fault, and that if they die, it will be because they willingly die.

The substance of the text lies in the following observations:

- **Principle 1:** It is the unchangeable law of God that wicked people must turn or die.

- **Principle 2:** It is the promise of God that the wicked will live if they will simply turn.

- **Principle 3:** God takes pleasure in people's conversion and salvation, but not in their death or damnation. He would rather have them return and live than continue in their ways and die.

- **Principle 4:** This is a most certain truth that God has confirmed to them by His oath because He does not want people to doubt this truth.

- **Principle 5:** The Lord reinforces His commands and exhortations to the wicked to turn.

- **Principle 6:** The Lord lowers Himself to reason the case with unconverted sinners and to ask them why they will die.

- **Principle 7:** If the wicked will not turn after all this, it is not God's fault that they perish, but it is their own fault. Their own stubbornness and rebellion is the cause of their damnation. Therefore, they die because they choose to die. They refuse to turn.

Having introduced the text in these points, I will next briefly speak somewhat of each of them in order.

Principle 1

It is the unchangeable law of God that
wicked people must turn or die.

I f you will believe God, believe this: there is only one of these two ways for every wicked person: either conversion or damnation. I know that the wicked will hardly be convinced either of the truth or fairness of this. It is no wonder if the guilty quarrel with the law. Few people are inclined to believe that which they do not want to be true, and even fewer want that to be true that they perceive is against them.

However, arguing with the law or with the judge will not save the wrongdoer. Believing and following the law might have prevented his death, but denying and accusing it will only hasten it. If it were not so, a hundred people would bring their reason against the law for every person who would bring his reason to the law, and people would rather choose to give their reasons why they should not be punished than to hear the commands and reasons of their leaders that require them to obey. The law was not made for you to judge, but that you might be ruled and judged by it.

But if there is anyone so blind as to try to question either the truth or the justice of this law of God, I will briefly give you that evidence of both, which I think should satisfy a reasonable person.

I. If you doubt whether this is the Word of God or not, besides a hundred other texts, you may be satisfied by these few:

- *Verily I say unto you, except ye be converted and become as little children, ye shall not enter into the kingdom of heaven* (Matthew 18:3).

- *Verily, verily, I say unto thee, except a man be born again, he cannot see the kingdom of God* (John 3:3).

- *If any man be in Christ, he is a new creature; old things are passed away; behold, all things are become new* (2 Corinthians 5:17).

- *Ye have put off the old man with his deeds, and have put on the new man, which is renewed in knowledge after the image of him that created him* (Colossians 3:9-10).

- *Follow . . . holiness, without which no man shall see the Lord* (Hebrews 12:14).

- *So then they that are in the flesh cannot please God. . . . Now if any man have not the Spirit of Christ, he is none of his* (Romans 8:8-9).

- *For in Christ Jesus neither circumcision availeth anything, nor uncircumcision, but a new creature* (Galatians 6:15).

- *According to his abundant mercy [he] hath begotten us again unto a lively hope* (1 Peter 1:3).

- *Being born again, not of corruptible seed, but of*

incorruptible, by the word of God, which liveth and abideth forever (1 Peter 1:23).

- *Wherefore laying aside all malice, and all guile, and hypocrisies, and envies, and all evil speakings, as newborn babes, desire the sincere milk of the word, that ye may grow thereby* (1 Peter 2:1-2).

- *The wicked shall be turned into hell, and all the nations that forget God* (Psalm 9:17).

- *The LORD trieth the righteous, but the wicked . . . his soul hateth* (Psalm 11:5).

As I do not need to explain these texts that are so plain, so I do not think I need to add any of the many other similar verses. If you are someone who believes the Word of God, this is already enough to satisfy you that the wicked must be either converted or condemned. You are already convinced that you must either confess that this is true or plainly say that you will not believe the Word of God.

Once you come to the point where you will not believe the clear Word of God, there is not much hope for you. Look to yourself as well as you can, for it is likely you will soon be in hell. You would be ready to quickly oppose someone who would lie to you, and yet you dare to lie about God? However, if you plainly tell God that you will not believe Him, do not blame Him if He never warns you anymore, or if He forsakes you and gives you up as hopeless – for what good would it do to warn you if you will not believe Him?

Even if He would send an angel from heaven to you, it seems you would not believe. For an angel can only speak the Word of God, and if an angel would bring you any other gospel, you are

7

not to receive it, but are to *let him be accursed* (Galatians 1:8). Certainly no angel is to be believed before the Son of God, who came from the Father to bring us this doctrine. If He is not to be believed, then all the angels in heaven are not to be believed. If these are the terms on which you stand with God, I will leave you until He deals with you in a more convincing way. God has a voice that will make you hear.

Although He urges you to hear the voice of His gospel, He will make you hear the voice of His condemning sentence without a request. We cannot make you believe against your wills, but God will make you see against your wills.

Let us hear what reason you have why you will not believe this verse from God's Word that tells us that the wicked must be either converted or condemned. I know your reason: it is because you think it is unlikely that God would be so unmerciful. You think it is cruelty to condemn people everlastingly for such a small thing as a sinful life. This leads us to the next point.

The fairness of God in His laws and judgments is justified.

II. The fairness of God in His laws and judgments is justified.

1. I do not think you will deny that it is most appropriate for an immortal soul to be ruled by laws that promise an immortal reward and threaten an endless punishment. Otherwise, the law would not be suited to the nature of the subject, who will not be fully ruled by any lower means than the hopes or fears of everlasting things. As it is in cases of worldly punishment, if a law were now made that the most heinous crimes would be punished with a hundred years' captivity, this might be of some effectiveness since the number of years is roughly equal to the years of our lives. But if there had been no other penalties before the flood, when people lived eight or

nine hundred years, it would not have been sufficient because people would know that they might have many hundred years of impunity afterward. It is the same in our present situation.

2. I suppose that you will admit that the promise of endless and inconceivable glory is not inappropriate to the wisdom of God or the case of man, so why, then, would you not think the same of the promise of endless and unspeakable misery?

3. When you find it in the Word of God that this is so, for so it is, do you think yourselves proper judges to contradict this truth? Will you call your Maker to the judgment seat and examine His word upon the accusation of falsehood? Will you sit over Him and judge Him by the law of your pride? Are you wiser, better, and more righteous than He? Must the God of heaven come to you to learn wisdom? Must Infinite Wisdom learn of folly, and Infinite Goodness be corrected, by a sinner who cannot keep himself pure and sinless for an hour? Must the Almighty stand at the judgment seat of a worm?

Oh, horrid arrogancy of senseless dust! Will a mole, or clump of dirt, or a dunghill accuse the sun of darkness and try to illuminate the world? Where were you when the Almighty made the laws without seeking your guidance? Surely He made them before you were born, and without desiring your advice. You came into the world too late to reverse them, if you could have done so great a work. You should have stepped out of your nothingness and contradicted Christ when He was on earth, or Moses before Him, or saved Adam and his sinful descendants from the threatened death so there might have been no need of Christ.

What if God would withdraw His patience and sustaining power and let you drop into hell while you are arguing with His Word? Will you then believe that there is a hell?

4. If sin is such an evil that it requires the death of Christ for its atonement, it is no wonder that it deserves our everlasting misery.

5. If the sin of demons deserves endless torment, why not also the sin of man?

6. I think you should understand that it is not possible for the best of people, much less for the wicked, to be competent judges of what is deserved for sin. We are both blind and partial. You can never fully know what sin deserves until you fully know the evil of sin, and you can never fully know the evil of sin until you fully know:

   a. The excellency of the soul that it damages.

   b. The excellency of holiness that it obliterates.

   c. The reason and excellency of the law that it violates.

   d. The excellency of the glory that it despises.

   e. The excellency and office of reason that it treads down.

   f. The infinite excellency, almightiness, and holiness of that God against whom it is committed.

When you fully know all these, you will fully know what sin deserves. Besides, you know that the offender is too partial to judge the law or the proceedings of his judge. We judge by feeling, which blinds our reason. In ordinary worldly things, we see that most people think that their own cause is right, and that whatever goes against them is wrong. It is in vain for even their most wise, just, or impartial friends to try to persuade them to the contrary. There are few children who do not think the father is unmerciful, or deals harshly with them, if he punishes them. There is hardly the vilest wretch who does not think that the church has done wrong if they excommunicate him. There is hardly a thief or murderer who is to be hanged who would not accuse the law and judge of cruelty, if doing so would benefit them.

7. Can you think that unholy souls should be in heaven? They cannot love God here or do Him any service that He can accept. They are contrary to God. They despise that which He most loves, and love that which He hates. They are incapable of that imperfect communion with Him that His saints partake of here. How, then, can they live in that perfect love of Him, and full delight and communion with Him, that is the blessedness of heaven? You do not accuse yourselves of not being unmerciful if you do not make your enemy your closest adviser, or if you do not allow your swine to live in your house with you, or even if you take away its life although it never sinned; yet you will blame the supreme Lord, the most wise and gracious Sovereign of the world, if He condemns the unconverted to perpetual misery.

I ask you now, all you who love your souls, that instead of quarrelling with God and with His Word, you will receive it now and use it for your good. All you who are still unconverted, accept this as the irrefutable truth of God. Before long, you must be either converted or condemned. There is no other way but to turn or die. When God, who cannot lie (Titus 1:2; Hebrews 6:18), has told you this, when you hear it from the Maker and Judge of the world – then it is time for those who have ears to hear.

By this time, you may see what you have to trust to. You are just dead and condemned people unless you will be converted. If I would tell you otherwise, I would be deceiving you with a

11

lie. If I would hide this from you, I would be doing you harm and would be guilty of your blood, as the verses preceding my text assure me: *When I say to the wicked man, O wicked man, thou shalt surely die; if thou dost not speak to warn the wicked from his way, that wicked man shall die in his iniquity; but his blood will I require at thine hand* (Ezekiel 33:8).

You see then, that although this is a rough and unwelcome doctrine, it is one that we must preach, and one that you must hear. It is easier to hear of hell than to feel it. If your necessities did not require it, we would not bother your tender ears with truths that seem so harsh and grievous. Hell would not be so full if people were only willing to know their situation and to hear and think of it. The reason why so few escape it is because they do not *strive to enter in at the strait gate* of conversion (Luke 13:24) and pursue the narrow way of holiness while they have time (Isaiah 35:8; Matthew 7:14).

They do not strive because they are not awakened to an active feeling of the danger they are in, and they are not awakened because they are reluctant to hear or think of it. That is partly through foolish sensitivity and carnal self-love, and partly because they do not really believe the message from God that tells of these truths. If you will not completely believe this truth, I think that the significance of it should force you to remember it, and it should stay with you and give you no rest until you are converted.

"You must be converted or condemned; turn, or die." If you had only once heard this message from the voice of an angel, would it not sink into your mind and torment you night and day? In your sinning, you would remember it as if the voice were still in your ears: "Turn or die!" Your soul would be happy if it could work with you in this way and never be forgotten and would never leave you alone until it has driven your heart home to God. However, if you will cast it out by forgetfulness or unbelief, how can it work to bring about your conversion and salvation? Remember this to your sorrow: although you may put this out of your mind, you cannot put it out of the Bible. It will stand there as a sealed truth that you will know by experience forever that there is no other way but to turn or die.

Oh, why are the hearts of sinners not pierced with such a solemn truth? We would think now that every unconverted person who hears these words would be pricked to the heart and think within himself, "This is my own situation," and never stop until he found himself converted. You may rightly believe that this drowsy, careless attitude will not last long. Conversion and condemnation are both awakening things, and you will experience one of them before long. As truly as if I saw it with my own eyes, I can predict that either grace or hell will soon bring these matters to the point and will make you say, "What have I done? What a foolish, wicked path I have taken!"

The scornful and foolish state of sinners will only last a little while. As soon as they either turn or die, the foolhardy dream will be at an end, and then their senses and feeling will return.

I foresee two things that are likely to harden the unconverted and make me lose all my labor unless they can be taken out of the way, and that is the misunderstanding of those two words – the *wicked* and *turn*. Some will think within themselves, "It is true that the wicked must turn or die, but that is not relevant to me. I am not wicked, even though I am a sinner, as all people are." Others will think, "It is true that we must turn from our evil ways, but I turned a long time ago. I have hope that I do not need to do this now."

And so while wicked people think they are not wicked, but are already converted, we lose all our labor in trying to persuade them to turn. Therefore, before I go any further, I will tell you here who are meant by the wicked, or who must turn or die. I will also explain what is meant by turning, or who are truly converted. I have purposely reserved this for this place, preferring the method that fits my purpose.

Who are the wicked, and what does it mean to turn?

I. You may observe here that in the sense of the text, a wicked person and a converted person are contraries. No person who is converted is a wicked person, and no person who is wicked is a converted person. To be a wicked person and to be an unconverted person is the same. Therefore, in dealing with one, we will deal with both.

Before I can tell you what either wickedness or conversion is, I must get back to the basics and take up the matter from the beginning.

It pleased the great Creator of the world to make three types of living creatures. He made angels pure spirits without flesh, and therefore He made them only for heaven and not to dwell on earth. Animals were made flesh without immortal souls, and therefore they were made only for earth and not for heaven. Man is of a middle nature, between both, as partaking of both flesh and spirit, and therefore he was made for both heaven and earth.

However, as his flesh is made simply to be a servant to his spirit, so he is made for earth simply as his passage or way to heaven, and not that this should be his home or happiness. The blessed state that man was made for was to behold the glorious majesty of the Lord and to praise Him among His holy angels, to love Him, and to be filled with His love forever. Since this was the purpose for which man was made, God gave him the means that were appropriate for him to attain it.

These means were principally two: (1) the proper inclination and disposition of the mind of man, and (2) the proper ordering of his life and practice. For the first, God adapted the disposition of man unto His purpose, giving him such knowledge of God as was appropriate for his present state, as well as a heart that was disposed and inclined to God in holy love. However, He did not secure or confirm him in this condition, but, having made him a free agent, He allowed him to exercise his own free will. For the second, God did that which belonged to Him. That is, He gave him a perfect law that required him to continue in the love of God and to perfectly obey Him.

By the deliberate transgression of this law, man not only forfeited his hope of everlasting life, but he also turned his heart from God and set it on these lower things of the flesh. In doing so, he blotted out the spiritual image of God from his soul. Man fell short of the glory of God, which was his purpose, and also took himself out of the way by which he could have attained it, and he did so as to the condition of both his

> Man did not live for God, but lived for his carnal self.

heart and his life. He lost the holy inclination and love of his soul to God, replacing it with an inclination and love to please his flesh, or carnal self, by earthly things, growing unfamiliar to God and familiar with the creature.

The direction of his life was suited to the bent and inclination of his heart. He did not live for God, but lived for his carnal self. He sought to please his flesh instead of seeking to please the Lord. We are all now born into the world with this nature or corrupt inclination, for *who can bring a clean thing out of an unclean?* (Job 14:4). As a lion has a fierce and cruel nature before it devours, and an adder has a venomous nature before it bites, so in our infancy we have those sinful natures or tendencies before we think or speak or do wrong. All the sin of our lives springs from this, and not only so, but when God, from His mercy, has provided us a solution, even the Lord Jesus Christ to be the Savior of our souls and bring us back to

God again, we naturally love our current condition and are reluctant to be brought out of it.

Therefore, we are set against the means of our recovery. Although custom has taught us to thank Christ for His goodwill, our carnal self convinces us to refuse His solution, and to desire to be excused when we are commanded to take the remedy that He offers and to forsake all and follow Him to God and glory.

I urge you to read over this section again, and pay attention to it, for in these few words you have a true description of our natural condition, and consequently of a wicked person, for every person who is in the state of corrupt nature is a wicked person and is in a state of death.

What does it mean to be converted?

II. Now you are prepared to understand what it means to be converted. To this end, you must also know that God in His mercy, not willing that man should perish in his sins, provided a solution by causing His Son to take our nature, and being in one person God and man, to become a mediator between God and man. By dying for our sins on the cross, He ransomed us from the curse of God and the power of the devil.

Having thus redeemed us, the Father has delivered us into His hands as His own. In doing so, the Father and the Mediator made a new law and covenant for man, not like the first, which gave life to none except the perfectly obedient, and which condemned man for every sin, but Christ has made a law of grace, or a promise of pardon and everlasting life, to all who by true repentance and by faith in Christ are converted unto God – like an act of amnesty that is made by a prince to a group of rebels on condition that they will lay down their arms and come in and be loyal subjects from then on.

However, because the Lord knows that the heart of man is so wicked that despite all this, people will not accept the remedy if they are left to themselves, therefore the Holy Spirit has undertaken it as His role to inspire the apostles, to seal the Scriptures by miracles and wonders, and to illuminate and convert the souls of the elect.

By this you can see that as there are three persons in the Trinity – the Father, the Son, and the Holy Spirit – so each of these persons have their specific works that are prominently connected to them.

The Father's works were to create us; to rule us, as His rational creatures, by the law of nature, and to judge us by that law; to provide us a Redeemer in His mercy when we were lost; and to send His Son and accept His ransom.

The works of the Son for us were to ransom and redeem us by His sufferings and righteousness; to give out the promise or law of grace, and to rule and judge the world as the Redeemer on those terms of grace; to make intercession for us so that the benefits of His death may be imparted; and to send the Holy Spirit, which the Father also does by the Son.

The works of the Holy Spirit for us are to compose the Holy Scriptures by inspiring and guiding the prophets and apostles; by sealing the Word by His miraculous gifts and works; by enlightening and inspiring the ordinary ministers of the gospel, and so enabling them and helping them to proclaim that Word; and by the same Word to enlighten and convert the souls of men. Just as you could not have been intelligent creatures if the Father had not created you, nor could you have had any access to God if the Son had not redeemed you, so neither can you have a part in Christ or be saved unless the Holy Spirit sanctifies you.

> The works of the Son for us were to redeem us by His sufferings and righteousness.

By now you may see the different details of this work. The Father sends the Son; the Son redeems us and makes the promise of grace; the Holy Spirit composes and seals this gospel; the apostles are the secretaries of the Spirit to write it; the preachers of the gospel proclaim it and persuade people to obey it; and the Holy Spirit makes their preaching effective by opening people's hearts to contemplate it. All this is to repair the image of God upon the soul, to set the heart upon God again, and to take it off the creature and carnal self to which it revolted, thereby turning the direction of the life into a heavenly path, that before was earthly. This is all done through embracing Christ by faith, for He is the Physician of the soul.

By what I have said, you may see what it means to be wicked and what it means to be converted. I think this will be even more clear to you if I describe them as consisting of their various parts.

A wicked person may be known by these three things:

1. He is one who places his main affections on earth. He loves the creature more than God, and his fleshly prosperity above heavenly joy. He savors the things of the flesh, but neither discerns nor savors the things of the Spirit. Although he will say that heaven is better than earth, yet he does not really regard it as such to himself. If he could be sure of earth, he would let go of heaven, and he would rather stay here than be taken there. A life of perfect holiness in the sight of God, dwelling in His love and praising Him forever in heaven, is not as pleasing to his heart as a life of health, wealth, and honor here upon earth. Although he falsely professes that he loves God above everything else, yet indeed he never felt the power of divine love within him, but his mind is more set on the world or fleshly pleasures than on God. In a word, whoever loves earth above heaven, and fleshly prosperity more than God, is a wicked, unconverted person.

On the other hand, a converted person is enlightened to

discern the loveliness of God. He so much believes the glory that is to be had with God that his heart is taken up with it and focused more upon it than on anything in this world. He would rather see the face of God and live in His everlasting love and praises than to have all the wealth or pleasures of the world. He sees that everything else is vanity, and that nothing can fill the soul except God. Therefore, no matter which way the world goes, he lays up his treasures and hope in heaven, and for that he is resolved to let everything else go.

As the fire ascends upward, and the needle of the compass turns to the north, so the converted soul is inclined unto God. Nothing else can satisfy him, nor can he be content or find any rest except in His love. In a word, all who are converted esteem and love God more than all the world, and the heavenly joy is dearer to them than their worldly prosperity.

The proof of what I have said may be found in the following passages of Scripture: Philippians 3:8-10; Matthew 6:19-21; Colossians 3:1-4; Romans 8:5-9, 18, 23; and Psalm 73:25-26.

2. A wicked person is one who makes it the main business of his life to prosper in the world and attain his worldly goals.

Although he may read, hear, and do much in the outward duties of religion, and refrain from disgraceful sins, yet this is all in passing, and he never makes it the main business of his life to please God and attain everlasting glory. Rather, he tries to appease God with the scraps of the world, and gives Him no more service than the flesh can spare, for he will not part with all of it for heaven.

On the contrary, a converted person is one who makes it the main care and business of his life to please God and to be saved, and takes all the blessings of this life only as that which helps him on his journey toward another life. He uses what he has in subjection to God. He loves a holy life, and desires to be more holy. He has no sin that he does not hate, and he longs and prays and strives to be rid of it. The direction and leaning of his life is for God, and if he sins, it is contrary to the very inclination of his heart and life. Therefore, he rises again and laments it, and dares not intentionally live in any known sin. There is nothing in this world so dear to him that he cannot give it up to God and forsake it for Him and the hope of glory.

You may see all this in Colossians 3:1-5; Matthew 6:20, 33; Luke 12:21; Luke 18:22-23, 29; Luke 14:18, 24, 26-27; Romans 8:13; Galatians 5:24, etc.

3. The soul of a wicked person never truly discerned and cherished the mystery of redemption, nor thankfully welcomed an offered Savior. Nor is he consumed with the love of the Redeemer, nor willing to be ruled by him as the Physician of his soul so that he may be saved from the guilt and power of his sins and restored to God. His heart is indifferent of this unspeakable benefit, and is quite against the healing means by which he should be restored. Although he may be willing to be outwardly religious, yet he never surrendered his soul to Christ and to the motions and conduct of His Word and Spirit.

On the contrary, the converted soul having felt himself ruined by sin, perceiving that he has lost his peace with God and the hope of heaven, and knowing that he is in danger of everlasting misery, thankfully welcomes the tidings of redemption.

Believing in the Lord Jesus as his only Savior, he surrenders himself to Him for wisdom, righteousness, sanctification, and redemption (1 Corinthians 1:30). He takes Christ as the life of his soul. He lives by Him and uses Him as a salve for every wound, admiring the wisdom and love of God in His wonderful work of man's redemption. In a word, Christ dwells in his heart by faith, and the life that he now lives is by the faith of the Son of God, who loved him and gave Himself for him. Yes, it is not so much he who lives, as Christ who lives in him. This can be seen in passages such as John 1:11-12; John 3:19-20; John 15:2-4; Romans 8:9; 1 Corinthians 1:30; 2:2; Galatians 2:20; and Philippians 3:7-10.

You see now in plain terms from the Word of God who are the wicked and who are the converted. Ignorant people think that if a person is not a swearer, a curser, a complainer, a drunkard, a fornicator, or an extortioner; if he deals honestly in his business; and if he goes to church and says his prayers, he cannot be a wicked person. Or they think that if someone who has been guilty of drunkenness, swearing, gambling, or similar vices simply abstains from them for now, they think this is a converted person. Others think if someone who has been an enemy of and ridiculed godliness now approves of it, joins himself to those who are godly, and is hated for it by the wicked, as the godly are, that this person must be converted.

Some people are so foolish as to think that they are converted by taking up some new and false belief, and joining with some fragmented religious group. Some people think that if they have simply been alarmed by the fears of hell and have had convictions of conscience, and thereupon have purposed and promised to change their lives, and have taken up a life of civil behavior and outward religion, that this must be true conversion.

These are the poor misguided and deceived souls who are likely to lose the benefit of all our attempts to persuade them to the truth. When they hear that the wicked must turn or die, they think that this is not spoken to them, for they do not think they are wicked, but have turned already. This is why Christ told some of the rulers of the Jews who were more solemn and ceremonial than the common people that *publicans and harlots go into the kingdom of God* before them (Matthew 21:31). It is not that a prostitute or flagrant sinner can be saved without conversion, but Jesus said this because it was easier to make these flagrant sinners realize their sin and misery and the necessity of a change than the more formal type of people who deceive themselves by thinking that they are converted already when they are not.

Oh, reader, conversion is another kind of work than most are aware of. It is not a small matter to bring a worldly mind to heaven and to show man the gracious excellence of God until he is taken up in such love to Him that it can never be quenched. It is not a small matter to break the heart for sin and to cause him to run for refuge to Christ and thankfully embrace Him as the life of his soul. It is not a small matter to have the very direction and inclination of the heart and life changed so that a person renounces that which he took for his happiness, and places his joy where he never did before so that he does not live for the same purpose as he formerly did and is not motivated by the same ways of the world as he formerly was.

In a word, he who is in Christ *is a new creature: old things are passed away; behold, all things are become new* (2 Corinthians 5:17). He has a new understanding, a new will, and a new purpose. He has new sorrows, new desires, new love, and new delight. He has new thoughts, new speeches, new company (if possible), and new conversation.

Sin, that before was a joking matter with him, is now so

abhorrent and terrible to him that he runs from it as from death. The world, that was so lovely in his eyes, now appears to him as emptiness and aggravation. God, who was before neglected, is now the only happiness of his soul. Before, He was forgotten, and every lust and desire was preferred before Him; but now He is set next to the heart, and all things must give place to Him. The heart is absorbed with listening to and obeying Him. It is grieved when He hides His face, and never thinks itself well without Him.

Christ Himself, whom before he never thought much about, is now his only hope and refuge, and he lives upon Him as on his daily bread. He cannot pray without Him, nor rejoice without Him, nor think, speak, or live without Him. Heaven itself, that before was looked upon only as a tolerable substitute, which he hoped might be more pleasing to him than hell when he could no longer stay in the world, is now taken for his home, the place of his only hope and rest, where he will see, love, and praise that God who already has his heart. Hell, that before seemed only as a threat to frighten people from sin, now appears to be a real misery that is not to be ventured on or joked about.

The works of holiness, of which he was weary before and which he thought were unnecessary, are now both his recreation and his business. The Bible, which was before to him almost as a common book, is now as the law of God – as a letter written to him from heaven and signed with the name of the eternal Majesty. It is the standard of his thoughts, words, and deeds. The commands are binding, the threats are fearful, and the promises of it speak life to his soul.

The godly, who seemed to him just like other people, are now the most excellent and happy people on earth. The wicked, who were his close friends, are now his grief. He who could laugh at their sins is more ready now to weep for their sin and misery, and to say with those of old, *But to the saints that are in the earth, and to the excellent, in whom is all my delight* (Psalm 16:3). *In whose eyes a vile person is contemned; but he honoreth them that fear the* LORD. *He that sweareth to his own hurt, and changeth not* (Psalm 15:4). *For many walk of whom I have told you often, and now tell you, even weeping, that they are the enemies of the cross of Christ* (Philippians 3:18).

In short, he has a new purpose in his thoughts and a new way in his work, and therefore his heart and life are new. Before, his carnal self was his purpose, and his pleasure and worldly profit and credit were his way. Now God and everlasting glory are his purpose, and Christ, the Spirit, God's Word, His ordinances, holiness to God, righteousness, and mercy to others are his way. Before, self was the main ruler, to which the matters of God and conscience must bow and yield. Now God, in Christ, by the Spirit, Word, and ministry, is the main ruler, to whom both self and all the matters of self must yield.

This is not a change in one, two, or twenty points, but in the whole soul, and in the very purpose and leaning of one's life. A person may step out of one path into another, yet have his face pointing the same way, and be still going toward the same place; but it is another matter entirely to turn completely around and take a journey in the opposite way to a completely different place.

> He who before was addicted to himself is now, by sanctification, devoted to God.

That is the case here. A person may turn from drunkenness, forsake other blatant, disgraceful sins, and practice some duties of religion, yet still be going the same way as before, loving his carnal self above all, and still giving it the dominion of his soul. However, when he is converted, this self is denied and taken down, and God is set up. The converted person's face is turned the opposite way, and he who before was addicted to himself and lived to himself is now, by sanctification, devoted

24

to God and lives unto God. Before, he asked himself what he should do with his time, his talents, and his possessions, and he used them for himself. Now he asks God what he should do with them, and he uses them for Him. Before, he would try to please God only as far as might agree with the pleasures of his flesh and carnal self, but not to any great displeasure of them. Now he desires to please God no matter how much his flesh and self might be displeased. This is the great change that God will make upon all who will be saved.

You can say that the Holy Spirit is our sanctifier, but do you know what sanctification is? This is what I have now explained to you, and every man and woman in the world must have this, or they will be condemned to everlasting misery. They must turn or die.

Do you believe all this, or do you not? Surely you dare not say that you do not, for it is past all doubt or denial. These are not differences of opinion where one educated pious person is of one mind and another person is of another mind, or where one person says this and the other person says that. Every group among us that deserves to be called Christians are all agreed in what I have said, and if you will not believe the God of truth, and that in a case where every group and party believes Him, you are entirely inexcusable.

But if you do believe this, how is it that you live so quietly in an unconverted state? Do you think that you are converted? Can you find this wonderful change upon your souls? Have you been born again and made new'? Are not these strange matters to many of you, and things that you never felt within yourselves? You cannot tell the day or week of your change, or the very sermon that converted you, yet do you find that the work is done, that there is indeed such a change, and that you have such hearts as are before described?

Sadly, most people follow their worldly business and do not

trouble their minds with such thoughts. If they merely keep themselves from scandalous sins, and can say, "I am not immoral, nor a thief, nor a curser, nor a swearer, nor an alcoholic, nor an extortioner. I go to church and say my prayers," they think that this is true conversion and that they will be saved as well as any. No! You are foolishly cheating yourselves. This is too much contempt of endless glory, and too glaring neglect of your immortal souls. Can you make such light of heaven and hell?

Your body will soon lie in the dust, and angels or demons will soon seize upon your souls. Every person reading this will soon be among other company, and in another situation than they now are. You will dwell in these houses only a little longer. You will work in your shops and fields only a little longer. You will sit in these seats and dwell on this earth only a little longer. You will see with these eyes, hear with these ears, and speak with these tongues only a little longer – until the resurrection day – and do you try to get these thoughts out of your minds so as not to have to think about these truths?

Oh, what a place you will soon be in of either joy or torment! Oh, what a sight you will soon see in either heaven or hell! Oh, what thoughts will soon fill your hearts with unspeakable delight or unspeakable horror! What work you will soon be employed in either to praise the Lord with saints and angels, or to cry out with demons in unquenchable fire! Should all this be forgotten? This will all be endless and will be sealed up by an unchangeable decree. Eternity will be the measure of your joys or sorrows, and can this be forgotten? This is all true – most certainly true.

When you have gone up and down a little longer, and slept and awaked a few more times, you will be dead and gone, and you will find all that I now tell you to be true. Can you forget these things now? You will then remember that you had this call, and that this day, in this place, you were reminded of these things, and you will perceive them to be matters of a thousand times more importance than either you or I could imagine here; yet will they now be so much forgotten?

Beloved friends, if the Lord had not awakened me to believe and take these things to heart myself, I would have remained in a dark and selfish state, and would have perished forever; but since He has truly made me aware of them, it will compel me to be sympathetic toward you as well as to myself. If your eyes were so far opened as to see hell, and you saw your neighbors who were unconverted dragged there with hideous cries, even though they were people whom you considered to be honest people on earth and who themselves feared no such danger, such a sight would make you go home and think about it, and think again, and would make you warn everyone around you, as that lost man of the world desired to do who wanted to warn his brothers so that they did not end up in that place of torment (Luke 16:28).

Faith is a kind of sight. It is the eye of the soul, *the evidence of things not seen* (Hebrews 11:1). If I believe God, it is next to seeing, and therefore, I ask you to excuse me if I am half as earnest with you about these matters as if I had seen them. If I must die tomorrow, and it were in my power to come again from another world and tell you what I had seen, would you not be willing to hear me, and would you not consider and believe what I would tell you? If I could preach one sermon to you after I am dead, after I have seen what is done in the world to come, would you not want me to plainly speak the truth? Would you not crowd around me to hear me, and would you not take my words to heart?

Faith is a kind of sight. It is the eye of the soul.

However, this will not happen. God has His appointed way of teaching you by Scripture and ministers, and He will not cater to unbelievers so far as to send people from the dead to them and change His established way. If any man disapproves of the sun, God will not indulge him so far as to set up a clearer light.

Friends, I plead with you to regard me now as you would do if I would come back from the dead to you, for I can give you as full assurance of the truth of what I say to you as if I had been there and had seen it with my eyes. It is possible for someone from the dead to deceive you, but Jesus Christ can never deceive you. The Word of God, delivered in Scripture and sealed by miracles and holy workings of the Spirit, can never deceive you. Believe this, or believe nothing. Believe and obey this, or you are done for.

If ever you would believe the Word of God, and if ever you would care for the salvation of your souls, let me beg of you this reasonable request, and I plead with you to hear me. Remember what has been said, earnestly search your hearts, and say to yourselves the following:

Is this indeed true? Must I turn or die? Must I be converted or condemned? It is time for me, then, to look around me before it is too late. Oh, why did I not look into this before now? Why did I foolishly avoid or ignore so great a matter? Was I awake or in my senses? O blessed God, what a mercy is it that You did not cut off my life all this time – before I had any certain hope of eternal life!

God forbid that I should neglect this work any longer. What state is my soul in? Am I converted, or am I not? Was ever such a change or work done upon my soul? Have I been enlightened by the Word and Spirit of the Lord to see the abhorrence of sin, the need of a Savior, the love of Christ, and the excellences of God and glory? Is my heart broken or humbled within me because of my former life? Have I thankfully cherished my Savior and Lord who offered Himself with pardon and life for my soul? Do I hate my former sinful life and the remnant of every sin that is in me? Do I flee from them as my deadly enemies? Do I give myself up to a life of holiness and obedience to God? Do I love it and delight in it? Can I truly say that I am dead to the world and carnal self, and that I live for God and the glory that He has promised? Does heaven have more of my esteem and affection than earth? Is God dearest and highest in my soul?

I am sure that I once lived mainly for the world and the flesh and that I gave God nothing except some heartless services that could be spared from the world and that were the leftovers of the flesh. Is my heart now turned another way? Do I have a new direction and a new purpose, and a new course of holy desires and habits? Have I set my hope and heart in heaven? Is it the purpose, goal, and intent of my heart to get well to heaven, to see the glorious face of God, and to live in His everlasting love and praise? When I sin, is it against the normal inclination and desire of my heart? Do I conquer all obvious sins, and am I weary and willing to be rid of my weaknesses?

This is the condition of converted souls. This is how it must be with me, or I will perish. Is it really this way with me, or is it not? It is time to get this doubt resolved before the dreadful Judge resolves it. I am not such a stranger to my own heart and life that I cannot somewhat recognize whether I am thus converted or not. If I am not, it will not do me any good to flatter my soul with false conceits and hopes. I am resolved to deceive myself no longer, but to strive to truly know whether I am converted or not – so that if I am, I may rejoice in it, glorify my gracious Lord, and comfortably go on until I reach the crown; and if I am not, that I may set myself to beg and seek after the grace that would convert me that I may turn to Christ without any more delay.

If I find out that I am not on the narrow way, then by the help of Christ I may turn and find new life; but if I remain as I am until either my heart is forsaken of God in blindness and hardness, or until I am carried away by death, then it is too late.

There is no place for repentance and conversion then. I know it must be now or never.

It is my request to you that you will simply take a close look at your heart and examine it until you see, if you can, whether you are converted or not. If you cannot find it out by your own endeavors, then go to your minister if he is a faithful and experienced man, and ask for his assistance. The matter is of utmost importance. Do not let timidity or carelessness hinder you. Godly ministers are set over you to advise you for the saving of your souls, just as physicians advise you for the curing of your bodies.

Many thousands of people are eternally ruined because they think they are in the way to salvation when they are not, and they think they are converted when they have not been. Then when we call to them daily to turn, they go away as they came, thinking that this does not concern them. They think they are turned already, and they hope they will do well enough in the way that they are in – at least if they pick the most pleasant path and avoid some of the crooked steps – when sadly, all this time they live only to the world and flesh and are strangers to God and eternal life, and they are quite far from the way to heaven. This is all because we cannot convince them to spend a little time seriously thinking about their condition and to spend a few hours examining their situation.

Are there not many self-deceivers who hear me this day who have never spent one hour, or even a quarter of an hour, in all their lives examining their souls to try to determine whether they are truly converted or not? Oh, what a merciful God who will care for such wretches who do not care more for themselves – who will do so much to save them from hell and help them to heaven who will do so little for it themselves! If all who are on the way to hell and in the state of damnation only knew it, they would not dare to continue in it.

The greatest hope that the devil has of bringing you to damnation without being rescued is by keeping you blindfolded and ignorant of your condition, and making you believe that you may do well enough by continuing in the way that you are now in. If you knew that you were not in the path to heaven, but were lost forever if you would die as you are, would you dare to sleep another night in that condition? Would you dare to live another day in it? Could you cheerfully laugh or be happy in such a condition, not knowing if you will be taken away to hell in an hour?

Certainly it would constrain you to forsake your former company and direction, and to commit yourselves to the ways of holiness and the communion of the saints. Certainly it would drive you to cry out to God for a new heart, and to seek help from those who are capable of giving you wise counsel. Certainly you care that you are condemned and damned to hell.

I ask you to make it your business to understand your own condition and build upon solid ground.

Well, then, I urge you to immediately make inquiry into your heart. Give it no rest until you find out your condition so that if it is good, you may rejoice in it and continue in it; and if it is bad, you may immediately seek for salvation, as people who believe they must turn or die.

What do you say? Will you resolve and promise to take this much labor for your own soul? Will you now enter upon this self-examination? Is my request unreasonable? Your conscience knows it is not. Resolve, then, before you move, to examine yourself, knowing how much it concerns your soul. I urge you, for the sake of that God who commands you, at whose judgment seat you will soon appear, that you do not deny me this reasonable request. For the sake of your soul that must turn or die, I ask you not to deny me this request, but make it your business to understand your own condition and build upon solid ground. Determine to know whether you are truly converted or not, and do not risk your soul on a false sense of security.

Maybe you will say, "What if we find ourselves still unconverted – what do we do then?" This question leads me to my second principle, which will do much to answer this question, and to which I now proceed.

Principle 2

It is the promise of God that the wicked
will live if they will simply turn.

God promises that the wicked will live if they will only sincerely and fully turn. The Lord here declares that He takes pleasure in the wicked turning and living. Heaven is made as sure to the converted as hell is to the unconverted. Turn and live is as certain a truth as turn or die.

After we had cast ourselves away by sin, God was not obligated to provide us a Savior, nor to open a door of hope for us, nor to call us to repent and turn – but He has freely done so to magnify His mercy. Sinners, none of you will have reason to go home and say that I preach hopelessness to you. We do not shut the door of mercy against you. Oh, that you would not shut it against yourselves! We do not tell you that God will not have mercy on you even if you turn and are sanctified. When did you ever hear a preacher say such a thing?

You who criticize the preachers of the gospel by saying that they desire to keep you out of hell and that they preach hopelessness, tell me, if you can, when you ever heard any earnest man say that there is no hope for you, even if you repent and are converted. No, it is the direct opposite that we daily proclaim from the Lord – that whoever is born again, and by faith and repentance becomes a new creature, will certainly be saved. We are so far from trying to convince you to despair of this that we try to convince you not to make any doubt of it.

It is not death, but life that is the first part of our message to you. Our duty is to offer salvation, certain salvation, a speedy, glorious, everlasting salvation to every one of you – to the poorest beggar as well as the greatest lord – to the worst of you, even to drunkards, swearers, thieves, those devoted to this world, and even to those who despise and reproach the holy way of salvation.

We are commanded by our Lord and Master to offer you a pardon for all that is past – if you will only now at last return and live. We are commanded to implore you and plead with you to accept the offer and return. We are to tell you what preparation is made by Christ, what mercy remains for you, what patience waits on you, what thoughts of kindness God has toward you, and how happy, how certainly and unspeakably happy, you may be if you will turn.

We also have indeed a message of wrath and death. Yes, it is a twofold wrath and death, but neither of them is our main message. We must tell you of the wrath that is on you already, as well as the death that you are born under for the violation of the law of works. However, this is only to show you the need of mercy and to encourage you to regard the grace of the Redeemer. You must know that we tell you nothing but the truth, for who will look for medicine who does not know that he is sick? Our telling you of your misery is not that which makes you miserable, but it should motivate you to seek for mercy. You have brought this death upon yourselves. We tell you also of another death, one that has no remedy and has much greater torment, that will fall on those who will not be converted.

However, since this is true and must be told to you, it is the last and saddest part of our message. We are first to offer you mercy – if you will turn. It is only those who will not turn or who refuse to hear the voice of mercy whom we must warn of their future damnation. If you will only cast away your transgressions, if you will delay no longer, but will come away at the call of Christ and be converted and become new creatures, then we do not have a word of damning wrath or death to speak against you.

In the name of the Lord of Life, I proclaim to all of you who hear me this day – to the worst of you, to the greatest, to the oldest sinner – that you may have mercy and salvation if you will only turn. There is mercy in God. There is sufficiency in the atonement of Christ. The promise is free, full, and universal. You may have life if you will only turn.

As you love your souls, remember what turning it is that the Scripture speaks of. It is not to mend the old house, but to pull it down and build anew on Christ, the Rock and our sure foundation. It is not to change a little in a carnal course of life, but to subdue the flesh and live after the Spirit. It is not to serve the flesh and the world in a more reformed way without any scandalous, disgraceful sins, and with a certain kind of religiousness; but it is to change your master, your works, and your purpose, and to set your face in the opposite way and do all for the life that you never saw. It is to dedicate yourselves and all you have to God. This is the change that must be made if you will live.

You are witnesses now that it is salvation, and not damnation, that is the great doctrine I preach to you and that is the first part of my message to you. Accept this, and we will go no farther with you, for we do not want so much as to frighten or trouble you with the name of damnation without necessity.

However, if you will not be saved, there is no remedy, but damnation must take place, for there is no middle place between the two. You must have either life or death.

> If you will not be saved, there is no remedy, but damnation must take place, for there is no middle place between the two.

Not only are we to offer you life, but we are to show you the basis on which we do it, and we call you to believe that God does indeed mean what He says. We tell you that the promise is true, that it extends conditionally to you, as well as to others, and that heaven is not merely a product of imagination, but it is a true place of delight.

If you ask where our authorization is for this offer, I will show it to you in a few texts of Scripture among a hundred. You see it here in my text and in the following verses. You see it in Ezekiel 18 as plainly as it can be spoken. In 2 Corinthians 5:17-21, you have the very sum of our commission:

If any man be in Christ, he is a new creature: old things are passed away; behold, all things are become new. And all things are of God, who hath reconciled us to himself by Jesus Christ, and hath given to us the ministry of reconciliation; to wit, that God was in Christ reconciling the world unto himself, not imputing their trespasses to them, and hath committed unto us the word of reconciliation. Now then, we are ambassadors for Christ, as though God did beseech you by us: we pray you in Christ's stead, be ye reconciled unto God. For he hath made him to be sin for us, who knew no sin; that we might be made the righteousness of God in him.

This is clear in the following passages as well:

Go ye into all the world, and preach the gospel to every creature. He that believeth [that is, with such a converting faith as is expressed] and is baptized shall be saved; and he that believeth not shall be damned. (Mark 16:15-16)

Thus it behooved Christ to suffer, and to rise from the dead the third day; and that repentance [which is conversion] and remission of sins should be preached in his name among all nations. (Luke 24:46-47)

The God of our fathers raised up Jesus, whom ye slew and hanged on a tree. Him hath God exalted with his right hand, to be a Prince and a Savior, for to give repentance to Israel, and forgiveness of sins. (Acts 5:30-31)

Be it known unto you therefore, men and brethren, that through this man is preached unto you the forgiveness of sins; and by him all that believe are justified from all things, from which ye could not be justified by the law of Moses. (Acts 13:38-39)

This offer is not just limited to the Jews.

For in Christ Jesus neither circumcision availeth anything, nor uncircumcision, but a new creature. (Galatians 6:15)

Come, for all things are now ready. (Luke 14:17)

By now you see that we are commanded to offer life to you all, and to tell you from God that if you will turn, you may live.

You may safely trust your souls to this, for the love of God is the foundation of this offer (John 3:16), and the blood of the Son of God has purchased it. The faithfulness and truth of God are pledged to make the promise good. Miracles often measure the truth of it. Preachers are sent throughout the world to proclaim it. The Spirit opens the heart to consider it, and the Holy Spirit Himself is the pledge of the full possession. The truth of this is past controversy, that the worst of you, and every one of you, may be saved if you will only be converted.

Indeed, if you choose to believe that you will be saved without conversion, then you believe that which is not true, and if I would preach that to you, I would be preaching a lie. You would not be believing God, but you would be believing the devil and your own deceitful hearts. God has His promise of life, and the devil has his promise of life. God's promise is, "Turn and live." The devil's promise is, "You will live whether you turn or not."

As I have shown you, the words of God are:

Except ye be converted and become as little children, ye shall not enter into the kingdom of heaven. (Matthew 18:3)

Except a man be born again, he cannot see the kingdom of God. (John 3:3)

Except a man be born of water and of the Spirit, he cannot enter into the kingdom of God. (John 3:5)

Without holiness, no man shall see the Lord. (Hebrews 12:14)

The devil's word is, "You may be saved without being born again and converted. You may get to heaven well enough without being holy. God is only trying to scare you. He is more merciful than to do what He says. He will be better to you than that."

Sadly, the majority of the world believes this word of the devil more than the Word of God, just as our sin and misery first came into the world. God said to our first parents, "If you eat, you will die" (Genesis 2:17), and the devil contradicted Him and said, "You will not die" (Genesis 3:4) – and the woman believed the devil more than God.

The Lord now says, "Turn or die," and the devil says, "You will not die. You just have to ask for God's mercy at the end and give up your sin when you can no longer engage in it." And this is the word that the world believes. Oh, such heinous wickedness to believe the devil more than God!

Yet that is not the worst. They blasphemously call this believing and trusting in God when they put Him in the shape of Satan, who was a liar from the beginning (John 8:44). When they believe that the Word of God is a lie, they call this trusting God, and they say they believe in Him and trust in Him for salvation. Where did God ever say that the unregenerate, unconverted, and unsanctified will be saved? Show me such a word in Scripture. I challenge you to do it. It is not there, for this is the devil's word, and to believe it is to believe the devil. This is the sin that is commonly called presumption, yet they call this believing and trusting in God. There is enough in the Word of God to comfort and strengthen the hearts of the sanctified, but not a word to strengthen the hands of wickedness or to give people the least amount of hope of being saved even though they have never been saved and set free from sin.

> There is enough in the Word of God to comfort and strengthen the hearts of the sanctified, but not a word to strengthen the hands of wickedness.

But if you will turn and come into the way of mercy, the mercy of the Lord is ready to welcome you. Boldly and confidently, then, trust God for salvation, for He is pledged by His word to save you. He will be a father to none except His children, and He will save none except those who forsake the world, the devil, and the flesh and come into His family to be members of His Son and have communion with His saints.

However, if they will not come in, it is their own fault. His doors are open. He does not keep anyone back. He never sent such a message as this to any of you: "It is now too late. I will not receive you, even though you are converted." He could have done so and would have done you no wrong, but He did not – and He does not to this day. He is still ready to receive you if you were simply sincerely ready to turn with all your heart.

The fullness of this truth will appear even more in the two following principles, to which I will therefore now proceed.

Principle 3

God takes pleasure in people's conversion and
salvation, but not in their death or damnation.
He would rather have them return and live than
continue in their ways and die.

The apostle Peter says that the Lord *is longsuffering to us-*
ward, not willing that any should perish, but that all should
come to repentance (2 Peter 3:9). He sincerely desires the conversion of all people. He does not, though, act as absolute Lord
as to use the fullest extent of His power to accomplish this, nor
as something that He resolves will undoubtedly come to pass
or would take all His power to accomplish.

A prince has the power to assign a guard to a murderer to
see that he will not murder and be hanged. However, if he does
not do so for a good reason, and simply sends messengers to
his subjects to warn them and plead with them not to be murderers, he may well say that he does not want them to murder
and be hanged. He takes no pleasure in it, but rather desires
them not to murder and to live. If he does happen to do more
for some people for some special reason, he is not obligated to

do the same for all. The king may well say to all murderers and felons in the land, "I have no pleasure in your death, but rather that you would obey my laws and live; but if you will not; I am resolved, for all this, that you will die." The judge may truly say to the murderer, "Alas, I have no delight in your death. I wish you would have kept the law and saved your life; but since you have not, I must condemn you, or else I would be unjust."

Although God has no pleasure in your damnation, and therefore calls upon you to return and live, yet He has pleasure in the demonstration of His own justice and the execution of His laws. Therefore, He is fully resolved that if you will not be converted, you will be condemned. If God were so much against the death of the wicked that He were resolved to do all that He can to prevent it, then no one would be condemned, yet Christ tells you that *narrow is the way that leadeth unto life, and few there be that find it* (Matthew 7:14). God is so much opposed to your damnation that He will offer you your choice, and command His ministers to plead with you.

God is so much opposed to your damnation that He will teach you, warn you, *set before you life and death* (Deuteronomy 30:19), offer you your choice, and command His ministers to plead with you not to destroy yourselves, but to accept His mercy, and so to leave you without excuse.

But if this will not do, and if you still remain unconverted, He declares to you that He is resolved on your damnation, and has commanded us to say to you in His name, *O wicked man, thou shalt surely die* (Ezekiel 33:8)! Christ has basically guaranteed over and over, with a *verily, verily*, that unless you are converted and born again, you cannot enter into the kingdom of heaven (Matthew 18:3; John 3:3). Notice that He says, *you cannot*. It is in vain to hope for it, and in vain to dream that God is willing for it, for it is something that cannot be.

You see the meaning of the text – that God, the great Lawgiver of the world, takes *no pleasure in the death of the wicked*, but rather that they turn and live, even though He is still resolved that none will live except those who turn. As a judge, He always delights in justice and in manifesting His hatred of sin, although considered in itself, He does not delight in the misery that sinners have brought upon themselves.

I will be brief in providing proof of this, for I suppose you easily believe it already.

1. The very gracious nature of God proclaimed this truth. *And the* LORD *passed by before him, and proclaimed, The* LORD, *the* LORD *God, merciful and gracious, longsuffering, and abundant in goodness and truth, keeping mercy for thousands, forgiving iniquity and transgression and sin, and that will by no means clear the guilty* (Exodus 34:6-7). This and many other passages may assure you that God has no pleasure in your death.

2. If God had more pleasure in your death than in your conversion and life, He would not have so often commanded you in His Word to turn. He would not have made you such promises of life for all who will simply turn. He would not have given so many reasons in trying to convince you to turn. The theme of His gospel proves the point.

3. His command and instruction that He has given to the ministers of the gospel fully prove it. If God had taken more pleasure in your damnation than in your conversion and salvation, He would never have told us to offer you mercy and to teach you the way of life, both publicly and privately. He would never have commanded us to beg you and plead with you to turn and live. He would not have instructed us to acquaint you with your sins and forewarn you of your danger. He would not

have told us to do all that we possibly can for your conversion, and to continue patiently in doing so, even though you would hate or abuse us for our efforts. Would God have done this, and appointed His ordinances for your good, if He had taken pleasure in your death?

4. It is proved also by the course of His providence. If God would rather have you damned than converted and saved, He would not second His Word with His works and allure you to Himself by His daily kindness. He would not give you all the mercies of this life, which are means to lead you to repentance (Romans 2:4). He would not bring you so often under His rod in order to bring you to your senses. He would not set so many examples before your eyes, nor wait on you as patiently as He does from day to day and year to year.

> If God would rather have you damned than saved, He would not allure you to Himself by His daily kindness.

These are not signs of one who takes pleasure in your death. If this had been His delight, He could have easily had you in hell long ago. He could have often cut you down in the midst of your sins while you had a curse or lie in your mouth, and when you were in your ignorance, pride, and carnality! When you were in your most recent drunkenness, or when you were lately mocking the ways of God, how easily He could have stopped your breath, restrained you with His afflictions, and made you comfortless in another world! How small a matter it is for the Almighty to silence the tongue of the most profane scorner, to tie the hands of the most malicious persecutor, or to calm the fury of the bitterest of His enemies and make them know that they are only worms!

If He would merely frown upon you, you would drop into your grave. If He gave a command to one of His angels to go and destroy ten thousand sinners, how quickly it would be done! How easily He can lay you upon the bed of sickness, make you lie there groaning in pain, make you eat the words of reproach that you have spoken against His servants, His word, His worship, and His holy ways, and make you beg the prayers of those whom you despised in your presumption! How easily He can bring pain and groaning to your body and make it too weak to hold your soul, making it more loathsome than the dung of the earth!

That flesh that now must have what it loves, and must not be displeased even if God is displeased; that flesh that must be indulged in food, drink, and clothing no matter what God says to the contrary – how quickly the displeasure of God could consume it! When you were passionately defending your sin and quarrelling with those who desired to draw you from it, when you were showing your anger against the reprover and pleading for the works of darkness – how easily God could have taken you away in a moment and set you before Him in His fearsome majesty, where you would see ten thousand times ten thousand glorious angels waiting upon His throne! He could have called you there to plead your case, and could have asked you: "What do you now have to say against your Creator, His truth, His servants, or His holy ways? Plead your case now, and make the best of it that you can. What can you now say in excuse of your sins? Give an account now of your worldliness and carnal life, of your time, and of all the mercies you have had."

Oh, how your stubborn heart would have melted, your proud look would have fled away, your countenance would have been terrified, and your tough words would have turned into speechless silence or dreadful cries if God had simply brought you before His judgment seat and pleaded His own case with you that you have here so maliciously pleaded against! How easily He can say at any time to your guilty soul, "Come away, and live in that flesh no more until the resurrection," and it cannot resist! One word from His mouth would destroy the poise of your present life, and then all your abilities and powers would stand still. If He would say to you, "Live no longer, or live in hell," you could not disobey.

However, God has not yet done any of this, but has patiently tolerated you, has mercifully upheld you, and has given you that breath that you breathed out against Him. He has given you those mercies that you sacrificed to your flesh, and He has granted you that provision that you used to satisfy your greedy throat. He gave you every minute of that time that you wasted in idleness, drunkenness, or worldliness.

Does not all His patience and mercy show that He did not desire your damnation? Can the candle burn without the oil? Can your houses stand without the earth to bear them? No, and you cannot live an hour without the support of God. Why did He support your life so long except to see when you would consider the folly of your ways, and return and live? Will any man purposely put weapons into his enemy's hands so the enemy can resist him, or hold a light for a murderer who is killing his children? Certainly God has waited so long for you in order to see whether you will at last turn and live.

5. It is further proved by the sufferings of His Son that God takes no pleasure in the death of the wicked. Would He have ransomed them from death at such an exorbitant cost? Would He have astonished angels and men by lowering Himself to come down to us? Would God have dwelt in flesh, come in the form of a servant, and assumed humanity into one person with the Godhead? Would Christ have lived a life of suffering and died a cursed death for sinners if He would have rather had taken pleasure in their death?

Suppose you saw Him as busy in preaching and healing of

the people as you find Him in Mark 3:20-21, or as long in fasting as in Matthew 4:2, or all night in prayer as in Luke 6:12, or praying with drops of blood trickling from Him instead of sweat as in Luke 22:44, or suffering a cursed death upon the cross and pouring out His soul as a sacrifice for our sins; would you have thought that these were the actions and signs of one who delighted in the death of the wicked?

Do not think to explain it away by saying that it was only for His elect, for it was your sin, and the sin of all the world, that lay upon our Redeemer, and His sacrifice and satisfaction is sufficient for all. The fruits of it are offered to one as well as another. It is true, though, that it was never the intent of His mind to pardon and save any who would not, by faith and repentance, be converted.

> It was your sin, and the sin of all the world, that lay upon our Redeemer, and His sacrifice is sufficient for all.

Would you have thought that He delighted in the death of the wicked, even of those who perish by their deliberate unbelief, if you had seen and heard Him weeping and grieving over the state of disobedience in unrepentant people?

> *And when he was come near, he beheld the city, and wept over it, saying, if thou hadst known, even thou, at least in this thy day, the things which belong unto thy peace! But now they are hid from thine eyes.* (Luke 19:41-42)

Would you have thought that He delighted in the death of the wicked if you had heard Him lamenting their stubbornness?

> *O Jerusalem, Jerusalem, . . . how often would I have gathered thy children together, even as a hen*

gathereth her chickens under her wings, and ye would not! (Matthew 23:37)

What if you had seen and heard Him on the cross praying for His persecutors?

Father, forgive them, for they know not what they do. (Luke 23:34)

When God so loved the world (not only loved, but so loved) as to give His only begotten Son, that whosoever believes in Him (by a living faith) *should not perish, but have everlasting life* (John 3:16), I think He proved by that, against the resentment of men and demons, that He takes no pleasure in the death of the wicked, but desires rather that they would turn and live.

6. If all this does not yet satisfy you, take His own word that He knows His own mind best, or at least believe His promise. This leads me to the fourth principle.

Principle 4

The Lord has confirmed to us by His word that
He has no pleasure in the death of the wicked,
but desires rather that they turn and live, for He
does not want to leave anyone with any excuse to
doubt this truth.

I f you dare to question His word, I hope you do not dare to
question His promise. As Christ has solemnly declared that
the unregenerate and unconverted cannot enter into the kingdom
of heaven (Matthew 18:3; John 3:3), so God has sworn that His
pleasure is not in their death, but in their conversion and life.

And as the Scriptures say, *because he could swear by no*
greater, he sware by himself (Hebrews 6:13).

For men verily swear by the greater: and an oath for
confirmation is to them an end of strife. Wherein
God, willing more abundantly to show unto the
heirs of promise the immutability of his counsel,
confirmed it by an oath; that by two immutable
things, in which it was impossible for God to lie, we

might have strong consolation, who have fled for
refuge to lay hold upon the hope set before us; which
hope we have as an anchor of the soul, both sure and
steadfast. (Hebrews 6:16-19)

If there is anyone who cannot reconcile this truth with the doctrine of predestination, or the actual damnation of the wicked, that is his own ignorance. He has no pretext left to question or deny the truth of the point in hand, for this is confirmed by the promise of God, and therefore must not be distorted to reduce it to other points. Rather, doubtful points must be reduced to it, and certain truths must be believed to agree with it, although our shallow minds hardly discern the agreement.

If you are an unconverted sinner who hears these words, I ask you now to ponder a little upon the previously mentioned principles, and think for a while who it is who takes pleasure in your sin and damnation. Certainly it is not God, for He has declared for His part that He takes no pleasure in it. I know that it is not your intention to please Him. You do not dare to say that you drink, swear, neglect holy duties, and quench the stirrings of the Spirit to please God. That would be like condemning the prince, breaking his laws, and seeking his death – and saying that you did all this to please him.

Who is it, then, who takes pleasure in your sin and death? It is not anyone who bears the image of God, for they must be like-minded to Him. God knows that your faithful teachers take no delight in seeing you serve your deadly enemy and recklessly risk your eternal state as you knowingly run into the flames of hell. It is no pleasure to them to see the sad effects of such blindness, hard-heartedness, carelessness, and presumption upon your souls. They take no joy in seeing such determination in evil and such unteachableness and stubbornness against the ways of life and peace.

They know these are marks of death and of the wrath of God, and they know, from the Word of God, what is likely to be the result of them. Therefore, it is no more pleasure to them than to a tenderhearted physician to see the marks of the plague break out upon his patient. How sad to foresee your everlasting torments, and not know how to prevent them; to see how near you are to hell, yet we cannot make you believe it and consider it; to see how easily, how certainly, you could escape, if we only knew how to make you willing! How near you are to everlasting salvation – if you would only turn and do your best and make it the care and business of your lives!

But you will not do it. Even though we give our lives to convince you of God's truth and your need of salvation, we cannot persuade you to it. We study day and night what to say to you that may convince and persuade you, and yet nothing has worked. We lay before you the Word of God, and show you the very chapter and verse where it is written that you cannot be saved unless you are converted, yet most of you remain unconverted. We hope you will believe the Word of God even if you do not believe us, and that you will pay attention to it when we show you the plain Scripture for it.

However, we hope in vain and labor in vain in regard to any saving change upon your hearts! Do you think that this is a pleasant thing to us? In secret prayer, we often lament to God with sad hearts:

O Lord, we have spoken to them in Your name, but they do not pay attention to us. We have told them what You commanded us to tell them concerning the danger of an unconverted condition, but they do not believe us. We have told them that You have said that there is no peace to the wicked (Isaiah 57:21), but even the worst of them will hardly believe that they are wicked. We have shown them Your Word, where You have said that if they live after the flesh, they will die (Romans 8:13), but they say that they will believe in You when they will not believe You. They say that they will trust in You when they give no credit to Your Word. They hope that the threatenings of Your Word are false, and they call that hoping in God. Although we show them where You have said that when a wicked man dies, all his hopes perish (Proverbs 11:7), yet we cannot persuade them to turn from their deceitful hopes.

We tell them what a contemptible, unprofitable thing sin is, but they love it, and therefore will not leave it. We tell them how much this pleasure will cost them, and that they must pay for it in everlasting torment; and they praise themselves and will not believe it, but will do as most people do. Because You are merciful, they will not believe You, but will imperil their souls, come what will. We tell them how ready You are to receive them, and this only makes them delay their repentance and be bolder in their sin.

> They hope that the threatenings of Your Word are false, and they call that hoping in God.

Some of them say they intend to repent, but they are still the same. Some say they have already repented, yet they are not converted from their sins. We warn them, we plead with them, and we offer them our help, but we cannot prevail with them. Those who were drunkards are still drunkards. Those who were carnal, flesh-pleasing reprobates are still the same. Those who were worldly are still worldly. Those who were ignorant and proud and self-conceited are still that way. Few of them will see and confess their sin, and fewer will forsake it, but they comfort themselves that all people are sinners, as if there were no difference between a converted sinner and an unconverted sinner.

Some of them will not come near us when we are willing to instruct them, but think they know enough already and do not need our instruction. Some of them will hear us, but then they do what they want. Most of them are like dead men who cannot feel, so that when we tell them of matters of everlasting consequence, we cannot get a word of it to their hearts. If we do not accept them in their sin and indulge them in doing all that they do, no matter how much against the Word of God it is, they will hate us and revile us. If we urge them to confess and forsake their sins, and save their souls, they will not do it. They would have us disobey God and condemn our own souls to please them, yet they will not turn and save their own souls to please You.

They are wiser in their own eyes than all their teachers. They rage and are confident in their own way, and no matter how concerned we are, we cannot change them.

Lord, this is the case of our pitiable neighbors, and we cannot help it. We see them ready to drop into hell, and we cannot help it. We know that they could be saved if they would sincerely turn, but we cannot prevail upon them to do so. If we would fall upon our knees and beg them, we cannot convince them to turn. If we would plead with them with tears to turn, we still cannot persuade them. What more can we do?

These are the secret complaints and laments that many poor ministers are compelled to make. Do you think that he has any pleasure in this? Is it a pleasure to him to see you continue in sin and not be able to stop you? Does it please him to see you so miserable and cannot even make you aware of it? Do you think he likes to see you lighthearted when you might be in hell within the hour? Does it give him pleasure to think what you must forever suffer because you will not turn, and to think what an everlasting life of glory you deliberately despise and cast away? What sadder thing can you bring to their hearts, and what else could you do to grieve them more?

Who is it, then, whom you please by your sin and death? You do not please any of your godly friends. No, for it grieves their souls to see your misery, and they often mourn for you when you do not thank them for it and when you do not have the heart to mourn for yourself.

Who is it, then, who takes pleasure in your sin?

1. **The devil** indeed takes pleasure in your sin and death, for this is the very goal of all his temptations. He watches for this night and day. You cannot please him any better than to continue in sin. How glad he is when he sees you going into the tavern, or committing some other sin, and when he hears you curse or swear or take God's name in vain! How glad he is when he hears you berate the minister who wants to draw you from your sin and help to save you! These things are his delight.

2. **The wicked** are also delighted in it, for it is agreeable to their nature.

3. Despite all this, I know that it is not the pleasing of the devil that you intend, even when you please him, but it is **your own flesh**, the greatest and most dangerous enemy, that you intend to please. It is the flesh that desires to be pampered and wants to be pleased in food and drink and clothing. It is your flesh that desires to be pleased with society, pleased in applause and honor from the world, and pleased in sports, lusts, and leisure. This is the gulf that devours all. This is the very god that you serve, for the Scripture says of such people that their bellies are their god (Philippians 3:19). Now I ask you to stay a little and consider the matter.

   a. **Question 1:** Should your flesh be pleased ahead of your Maker? Will you displease the Lord, your teacher, and your godly friends in order to please your carnal appetites or fleshly desires? Is not God worthy to be the ruler of your flesh? If He does not rule it, He will not save it. You cannot reasonably expect that He would.

b. **Question 2:** Your flesh is pleased with your sin, but is your conscience pleased? Is it not dissatisfied within you? Does it not tell you sometimes that all is not well and that your situation is not as safe as you make it to be? Should not your souls and consciences be pleased before your corruptible flesh?

c. **Question 3:** Is not your flesh preparing for its own displeasure also? It loves the bait, but does it love the hook? It loves the strong drink and sweet morsels; it loves its ease and sports and fun; it loves to be rich and well-spoken of by people, and to be somebody in the world; but does it love the curse of God? Does it love to stand trembling before His judgment seat and to be condemned and sentenced to everlasting fire? Does it love to be tormented with the demons forever?

Consider all of this, for there is no separating sin and hell except by faith and true conversion. If you will keep one, you must have the other. If death and hell are pleasant to you, it is no wonder that you continue in sin, but if they are not (as I am sure they are not), then no matter how pleasant sin seems to be, is it worth the loss of eternal life? Is a little

> Lord affirms that He has no pleasure in your death, but rather that you would turn and live.

drink, food, or ease worth losing your soul? Is the flattery of sinners or the riches of this world to be valued above the joys of heaven? Are they worth the sufferings of eternal fire? Before you go any further, these questions should be considered by every person who has sense to consider and who believes he has a soul to save or lose.

The Lord here affirms that He has no pleasure in your death, but rather that you would turn and live. If, however, you choose to continue as you are and to die rather than turn, remember that it was not to please God that you did it, but it was to please the world and to please yourself. If people will doom themselves to please themselves, if they choose to face endless torments for a little temporary delight, and if they do not have the sense, the heart, or the grace to listen to God or man who desire to redeem them, what remedy is there? They must take what they get by this, and repent of it in another manner – when it is too late!

Before I proceed any further in the application, I will consider the next doctrine, which gives me a more solid foundation for it.

Principle 5

The Lord reinforces His commands and exhortations to the wicked to turn.

God is so earnest for the conversion of sinners that He doubles His commands and exhortations with intensity: Turn ye, turn ye, from your evil ways; for why will ye die? (Ezekiel 33:11).

This principle is the application of the former principle, by way of exhortation, and that is how I will deal with it. Is there an unconverted sinner who hears these impassioned words of God? Is there a man or woman here who is still a stranger to the renewing, sanctifying work of the Holy Spirit? It is good if it is not so with most who are here. Listen, then, to the voice of your Maker, and turn to Him through Christ without delay.

Do you want to know the will of God? This is His will – that you immediately turn. Will the living God send so earnest a message to His creatures, and will they not obey?

Listen, then, all you who live after the flesh: the Lord who gave you your breath and being has sent a message to you from

57

heaven, and this is His message: *Turn ye, turn ye . . . ; for why will ye die?* He who has ears to hear, let him hear. Will the voice of the eternal Majesty be neglected? If He only thunders, you are afraid. Oh, but this voice more closely concerns you. If He only tells you that you will die tomorrow, you would not make light of it, but this word concerns your everlasting life or death.

It is both a command and an exhortation. It is as if He had said to you, "I command you, upon the allegiance that you owe to Me, your Creator and Redeemer, that you renounce the flesh, the world, and the devil and turn to Me so that you may live. I lower Myself to plead with you, as you either love or fear Him who made you, and as you love your own life, even your everlasting life: turn and live. If you want to escape eternal misery, turn, turn, for why will you die?"

Is there a heart in man, in a reasonable creature, who can ever refuse such a message, such a command, such an exhortation as this? If so, then what a thing is the heart of man!

Listen, then, all you who love yourselves, and all who regard your own salvation, for this is the most joyful message that was ever sent to the ears of man: *Turn ye, turn ye . . . ; for why will ye die?* You are not yet forever confined under desperation. Mercy is here offered to you. Turn, and you will have it. With what glad and joyful hearts you should receive these tidings! I know this is not the first time that you have heard it, but how have you regarded it, or how do you regard it now?

Hear the Word of the Lord, all you ignorant, careless sinners. Hear, all you who love the world, you carnal pleasers of the flesh, you gluttons, drunkards, immoral, and swearers; you blasphemers and backbiters, slanderers and liars: *Turn ye, turn ye . . . ; for why will ye die?*

Hear, all you cold and outward professors of the faith, and all who are strangers to the life of Christ. Hear, all you who never knew the power of His cross and resurrection, and never felt your hearts warmed with His love. Hear, you who do not abide in Him as the strength of your souls: *Turn ye, turn ye . . . ; for why will ye die?*

Hear, all who are barren of the love of God, whose hearts are not toward Him, nor taken up with the hopes of glory, but who put more value on your earthly prosperity and delights than on the joys of heaven. Hear, all you who are merely a little religious and give God no more than your flesh can spare. Listen, all you who have not denied your carnal selves and forsaken all that you have for Christ, but have something in the world so dear to you that you cannot spare it for Christ if He required it, but will rather risk His displeasure than forsake it: *Turn ye, turn ye . . . ; for why will ye die?*

If you never heard it or regarded it before, remember that you were told from the Word of God this day that if you will only turn, you may live – and if you will not turn, you will surely die.

What now will you do? What is your answer? Will you turn, or will you not? Do not waver any longer between two opinions. If the Lord is God, follow Him; if your flesh is your god, then serve it still (1 Kings 18:21). If heaven is better than earth and fleshly pleasures, then come away and seek *a better country* (Hebrews 11:16). Lay up your treasure where rust and moths do not corrupt, and where thieves cannot break through and steal (Matthew 6:20). Be awakened at last to seek with all your might the kingdom that cannot be moved (Hebrews 12:28). Apply your lives for a higher purpose, and turn the direction of your cares and labors another way than you have previously done.

However, if earth is better than heaven, or will do more for you, then keep it and make your best of it, and keep following it. Are you resolved what to do? If you are not, I will set a few more meaningful considerations before you to see if reason will make you decide.

I. Consider what preparations mercy has made for your salvation, and what a shame it is that anyone would be damned after all this. There was a time when the flaming sword was in the way, and the curse of God's law would have kept you back even if you had been very willing to turn to God. There was a time when you, and all the friends that you had in the world, could never have brought about the pardon of your past sins, no matter how much you had lamented and reformed them.

But Christ has removed this impediment by the ransom of His blood. There was a time when God was entirely unreconciled as being not satisfied for the violation of His law, but now He is so much satisfied and reconciled that He has offered you a full pardon and a free gift of Christ and life, and He offers it to you and urges you to accept it. It may be yours if you want it, for He was in Christ reconciling the world to Himself, and has committed to us the word of reconciliation (2 Corinthians 5:18-19).

Sinners, we are also commanded to deliver this message to you as from the Lord: *Come, for all things are now ready* (Luke 14:17). All things are ready, and are you unready? God is ready to receive you and to forgive all that you have done against Him if you will only come to Him. As often as you have sinned, as willingly as you have sinned, and as despicably as you have sinned, He is ready to cast it all behind His back if you will only come.

Although you have been prodigals, you have run away from God, and you have stayed away so long, He is still ready to meet you, to embrace you in His arms, and to rejoice in your conversion if you will only turn. Even worldly people and drunkards will find God ready to welcome them if they will simply come.

Does not this soften your heart within you? Oh, sinner, if you had a heart of flesh and not a heart of stone, it seems to me that this would melt it. Will the almighty, infinite Majesty of heaven wait for you to turn, and will He even be ready to receive you – you who have offended Him and forgotten Him for so long? Will He delight in your conversion that might at any time glorify His justice in your damnation? Does this not melt your heart within you, yet are you still not ready to come in? Do you not have as much reason to be ready to come as God has to invite you and welcome you?

But that is not all. Christ has died on the cross, and has made such a way for you to the Father that, because of Him, you may be welcome if you will come, yet are you not ready? A pardon is already plainly granted and offered to you in the gospel, yet are you not ready? The ministers of the gospel are ready to assist you, instruct you, and pray for you, yet are you not ready?

All who are around you who fear God are ready to rejoice in your conversion. They are ready to receive you into the communion of saints and to give you the right hand of fellowship, even though you had been one who had been cast out of their society. They willingly forgive where God forgives when it is clear to them by your confession and changed life. They dare not as much as rebuke you for your former sins, because they know that God will not denounce you for them. Even if you have been very evil, if you would simply wholeheartedly be converted and come in, they would not refuse you, no matter what the world would say against it. All these people are ready to receive you, yet are you not ready to come in?

Yes, heaven itself is ready. The Lord will receive you into the glory of His saints. As wicked as you have been, if you will only be cleansed, you may have a place before His throne. His angels will be ready to guard your soul to the place of joy if you only genuinely and sincerely come in. God is ready, the sacrifice of Christ is ready, the promise is ready, and pardon is ready. Ministers are ready, angels are ready, the people of God are ready, and heaven itself is ready. They are all only waiting for your conversion – yet are you not ready?

What! You are not ready to live when you have been dead so long? You are not ready to come to your right understanding, as the prodigal *came to himself* (Luke 15:17), when you have been beside yourself so long? Are you not ready to be saved when you are even ready to be condemned? Are you not ready to lay hold on Christ, who would deliver you, when you are even ready to sink into damnation? Are you not ready to be saved from hell when you are even ready to be cast into it without hope?

Do you know what you are doing? If you die unconverted, there will be no doubt of your damnation. You are not certain that you will even live another hour, yet are you not ready to turn and to come in? Oh, miserable wretch! Have you not served the flesh and the devil long enough? Have you not had enough of sin? Is it so good to you or so profitable for you? Do you know what it is and how destructive and abominable it is, yet you want more of it? Have you had so many calls, so many mercies, so many warnings, and so many examples? Have you seen so many laid in the grave, yet are you not ready to let go of your sins and come to Christ?

After so many convictions and pains of conscience, after so many purposes and promises, are you not yet ready to turn and live? Oh, that your eyes and heart were opened to know how good an offer is now made to you! What a joyful message it is that we are sent on, to call you to come – for all things are ready (Luke 14:17)!

II. Consider also what calls you have to turn and live. How many calls, how loud, how sincere, how alarming – yet what encouraging, joyful calls! The primary inviter is God Himself.

He who commands heaven and earth commands you to turn, and to do so immediately and without delay. He commands the sun to run its course and to rise upon you every morning; and though it is such a glorious heavenly body, and is many times bigger than all the earth, yet it obeys Him and does not fail even one minute of its appointed time. He commands all the planets and the spheres of heaven, and they obey. He commands the sea to ebb and flow, and commands the entire creation to keep its course, and all obey Him. The angels of heaven obey His will, even when He sends them to minister to such worms as we on earth (Hebrews 1:14); yet if He commands a sinner to turn, he will not obey Him. He thinks he is wiser than God. He complains and pleads the cause of sin, and will not obey. If the Lord Almighty says the word, the heavens and all therein obey Him, but if He calls a drunkard out of a tavern, he will not obey. If He calls a worldly, carnal sinner to deny himself, subdue the flesh, and set his heart upon a better inheritance, he will not obey.

If you had any love in you, you would know the voice, and you would say, "Oh, this is my Father's call! How can I find it in my heart to disobey? The sheep of Christ know and hear His voice and they follow Him, and He gives them eternal life" (John 10:4). If you had any spiritual life and sense in you, you would at least say, "This call is the mighty voice of God, and who would dare to disobey? For the prophet said, *The lion hath roared; who will not fear?*" (Amos 3:8).

God is not a man that you should delay and ignore Him and treat Him lightly. Remember what He said to Paul at his conversion: *It is hard for you to kick against the pricks* (Acts 9:5). Will you still go on and despise His Word, resist His Spirit, and stop your ears against His call? Who will have the worst of this? Do you know whom you disobey and contend with? Do you realize what you are doing? It would be much wiser and easier for you to contend with the thorns, walk on them with your bare feet, and crush them with your bare hands, or even to put your head into the burning fire. *Be not deceived.* God will not be mocked (Galatians 6:7). No matter who else is mocked, God will not be. It would be better for you to play with fire on your thatched roofs than with the fire of His burning wrath. *For our God is a consuming fire* (Hebrews 12:29).

Oh, how unsuitable a match you are for God! *It is a fearful thing to fall into the hands of the living God* (Hebrews 10:31). Therefore, it is a fearful thing to contend with Him or resist Him. If you love your own souls, take heed what you do. What will you say if He begins in wrath to contend with you? What will you do once He begins to deal with you? Will you then strive against His judgment as you now strive against His grace? God says, *Fury is not in me;* that is, He does not delight to destroy you. It is as if He does so almost unwillingly. He adds, *Who would set the briars and thorns against me in battle? I would go through them, I would burn them together. Or let him take hold of my strength, that he may make peace with me, and he shall make peace with me* (Isaiah 27:4-5). It is an unequal combat for the briers and thorns to make war with the fire.

You see who it is who calls you, who desires to move you to hear His call and turn. Consider also by what instruments, and how often, and how earnestly He calls.

1. Every page of the blessed Book of God has, as it were, a voice, and calls out to you: "Turn and live; turn, or you will die." How can you open it and read a page or hear a chapter and not understand that God desires you to turn?

64

2. It is the voice of every sermon that you hear, for what else is the scope and purpose of it all except to call, persuade, and entreat you to turn?

3. It is the voice of many movements of the Spirit that secretly speaks these words over again and urges you to turn.

4. It is likely sometimes the voice of your own conscience. Are you not sometimes convinced that all is not well with you? Does not your conscience tell you that you must be a new person and take a new direction in life, and does not it often call upon you to return?

5. It is the voice of the gracious examples of the godly. When you see them live a heavenly life and flee from the sin that is your delight, this really calls on you to turn.

6. It is the voice of all the works of God. They also are God's books that teach you this lesson by showing you His greatness, wisdom, and goodness, and by calling you to observe them and admire the Creator. *The heavens declare the glory of God, and the firmament showeth his handywork: day unto day uttereth speech, and night unto night showeth knowledge* (Psalm 19:1-2). Every time the sun rises unto you, it really calls you to turn, as if it is saying, "What do I travel and circle the world for except to declare to mankind the glory of their Maker, and to light them to do His work? And do I still find you doing the work of sin and spending your life in negligence?"

Awake, thou that sleepest, and arise from the dead, and Christ shall give thee light (Ephesians 5:14). *Now it is high time to awake out of sleep. . . . The night is far spent, the day is at hand; let us therefore cast off the works of darkness, and let us put on the armor of light. Let us walk honestly, as in the day; not in rioting and drunkenness, not in chambering and wantonness, not in strife and envying. But put ye on the Lord Jesus Christ, and make not provision for the flesh, to fulfil the lusts thereof* (Romans 13:11-14). This text was the means of Augustine's conversion.

7. It is the voice of every mercy you possess. If you could only hear and understand them, they all cry out to you, "Turn." Why does the earth bear you except to seek and serve the Lord? Why does it provide you its fruits except to serve Him? Why does the air give you breath except to serve Him? Why do all the creatures serve you with their labors and their lives except that you might devote them and yourself to the service of God? Why does He give you time, health, and strength except to serve Him? Why do you have food, drink, and clothing except for His service?

Do you have anything that you have not received (1 Corinthians 4:7)? If you did receive it, it is good for you to remind yourself from whom you received it, and to what purpose and use you received it. Did you ever cry to God for help in your distress, and did you not then understand that it was your part to turn and serve Him if He would deliver you? He has done His part and has spared you a while longer, and has given you another, and another year, and yet you do not turn.

You know the parable of the unfruitful fig tree (Luke 13:6-9). When the owner said, *Cut it down; why cumbereth it the ground?* he was asked to try it one year longer, and then if it did not prove fruitful, to cut it down. Christ Himself makes the application twice there: *Except ye repent, ye shall all likewise perish* (Luke 13:3, 5). How many years has God looked for the fruits of love and holiness from you, and has found none, yet He has spared you? How many times by your willing ignorance, carelessness, and disobedience have you provoked justice to say, "Cut him down; why does he cumber the ground?" Yet mercy has prevailed, and patience has delayed the fatal blow to this day. If you had understanding within you, you would know that all this calls you to turn.

Do you think you will still *escape the judgment of God? Or despisest thou the riches of his goodness and forbearance and longsuffering; not knowing that the goodness of God leadeth thee to repentance? But after thy hardness and impenitent heart, treasurest up unto thyself wrath against the day of wrath and revelation of the righteous judgment of God, who will render to every man according to his deeds* (Romans 2:3-6).

8. Moreover, it is the voice of every affliction to call you to make haste and turn. Sickness and pain cry, "Turn." Poverty, loss of friends, and every branch of the chastening rod cry, "Turn." Yet will you not listen to the call? These have come near you and have made you think. They have made you groan, and can they not make you turn?

9. The very fabric of your nature and being itself calls you to turn. Why do you have reason except to rule your flesh and serve your Lord? Why do you have an understanding soul except to learn and know His will and do it? Why do you have a heart within you that can love and fear and desire except that you should fear Him and love Him and desire after Him?

Put all these together now, and see what the issue should be. The Holy Scriptures call upon you to turn. The ministers of Christ call upon you to turn. The Spirit cries, "Turn." Your conscience cries, "Turn." The godly, by persuasion and example, cry, "Turn." The whole world, and all the creatures in the world that are presented to your consideration, cry, "Turn." The patient forbearance of God cries, "Turn." All the mercies that you receive cry, "Turn." The rod of God's chastisement cries, "Turn." Your reason and the very fabric of your nature calls you to turn. All your promises to God tell you to turn. Yet are you not resolved to turn?

III. Moreover, poor hard-hearted sinner, did you ever consider upon what terms you stand all this time with Him who calls on you to turn? You are His own, and you owe Him yourself and all that you have – and may He not command His own? You are His absolute servant, and you should serve no other master. You stand at His mercy, and your life is in His hand. He is resolved to save you upon no other terms.

You have many cruel spiritual enemies who would be glad if God would only forsake you, leave them alone with you, and leave you to their will. How quickly they would deal with you in another manner, yet you cannot be delivered from them except by turning to God. You have already fallen under His wrath by your sin, and you do not know how long His patience will still wait. This might be the last year – or the last day. His sword is even at your heart while the word is in your ear. If you do not turn, you are dead and done for. If only your eyes were open to see where you stand – even upon the brink of hell – and to see how many thousands are there already who did not turn, you would see that it is time to look around you.

> You stand at God's mercy, and your life is in His hand. He is resolved to save you upon no other terms.

Look inward now and tell me how your hearts are affected with these offers of the Lord. You hear what is in His mind. He does not delight in your death. He calls to you, "Turn, turn!" It is a fearful sign if all this does not move you, or if it only somewhat moves you – and much more if it makes you more careless in your misery because you hear of the mercifulness of God. The working of the medicine will partly tell us whether there is any hope of the cure.

Oh, what glad tidings it would be to those who are now in hell if they had such a message from God! What a joyful word it would be to hear this: "Turn and live!" Yes, what a welcome word it would be to yourself if you had felt that wrath of God for only an hour! It would bring hope and joy even if after a thousand or ten thousand years' torment, you could simply hear such a word from God: "Turn and live!" Yet will you neglect it and allow us to return without accomplishing our errand?

Behold, sinners, we are sent here as the messengers of the Lord to set before you life and death. What do you say? Which of them will you choose? Christ stands, as it were, by you, with heaven in the one hand and hell in the other, and He offers you your choice. Which will you choose? The voice of the Lord makes the rocks tremble (Psalm 29), and does it mean nothing to you to hear Him warn you of what will happen to you if you will not turn? Do you not understand and feel this voice that says, *Turn ye, turn ye . . . ; for why will ye die?*

It is the voice of love, of infinite love, of your best and kindest friend, as you might easily perceive by the invitation, yet can you neglect it? It is the voice of mercy and compassion. The Lord sees where you are going better than you do, which makes Him call after you, *Turn, turn.* He sees what will become of you if you will not turn. He thinks to Himself, "This poor sinner will cast himself into endless torments if he does not turn. I must deal with him in justice according to My righteous law." Therefore, He calls out to you, *Turn, turn.* Oh, sinner, if you only knew as well as God does even the thousandth part of the danger that is near you, and the misery that you are running into, we would have no more need to call after you to turn.

Moreover, this voice that calls to you is the same voice that has prevailed with thousands already. It has called all to heaven who are now there, and they would not now for a thousand worlds wish that they had made light of His call and not turned to God. What do those who have listened to God's call and have turned now enjoy? They now perceive that it was indeed the voice of love, a voice that did not desire their harm, but only their salvation. If you will obey the same call, you will come to the same happiness.

There are millions of people who will forever lament that they did not turn, but there is never a soul in heaven that is sorry that they were converted. Well, are you resolved to turn yet, or are you not? Do I need to say any more to you? What will you do? Will you turn or not? Speak in your heart to God, even if you do not speak out to me. Speak to Him so that He does not take your silence for denial. Speak quickly, for He may never make you the offer again. Speak resolutely and unwaveringly, for He does not want any halfhearted followers.

> There are millions who will forever lament that they did not turn, but there is never a soul in heaven that is sorry that they were converted.

Say in your heart now, without any more delay, even before you stand up, "By the grace of God, I am resolved right now to turn. Because I know my own insufficiency, I am resolved to wait on God for His grace, follow Him in His ways, forsake my former ways and companions, and give myself up to the guidance of the Lord."

You are not closed up in the darkness of heathenism or in the desperation of the doomed. Life is before you, and you may have it on reasonable terms if you want it. Yes, you can have it for free if you will accept it. The way of God lies plainly before you. The body of Christ is open to you. You may have Christ, pardon, and holiness if you desire.

What will you say? Will you or won't you? If you say no, or say nothing, and continue as you are, God is a witness, those who hear me are witnesses, and your own conscience is a witness how merciful and generous an offer you had this day. Remember – you could have had Christ, and you refused. When you have lost it, remember that you could have had eternal life as well as others, and you would not – and all this because you would not turn!

Let us now move on to the next principle and hear your reasons.

Principle 6

The Lord lowers Himself to reason the case with unconverted sinners and to ask them why they will die.

*T*his is a strange disputation, both regarding the controversy and the disputants.

1. The controversy or question proposed is why wicked people will destroy themselves, or why they choose to die rather than turn, and whether they have any sufficient reason for doing so.

2. The disputants are God and man – the most holy God and wicked, unconverted sinners.

I. Is it not a strange thing that God here seems to suppose – that anyone would be willing to die and be condemned, and that this would be the case of all the wicked? The wicked, the unconverted sinners, make up the majority of the world. But you will say that this cannot be, for nature desires its own preservation and joy, and the wicked are more selfish, not less selfish, than others. Therefore, how can anyone be willing to be damned?

There are two parts to my answer: (1) It is a certain truth that no one can be willing to bear any evil as evil, but only as it has some appearance of good; much less can anyone be willing to be eternally tormented. Misery, as such, is desired by none. (2) Yet despite that, it is most true that God teaches us here that the reason why the wicked die is because they choose to die. This is true in several respects.

1. The wicked die because they choose to go the way that leads to hell, even though they are told by God and man where it leads and where it ends, and even though God has so often declared in His Word that they will be condemned if they continue in that way and that they will not be saved unless they turn. *There is no peace, saith the LORD, unto the wicked* (Isaiah 48:22). *There is no peace, saith my God, to the wicked* (Isaiah 57:21). *The way of peace they know not; there is no judgment in their goings; they have made them crooked paths. Whosoever goeth therein shall not know peace* (Isaiah 59:8). They have the word and the promise of the living God for it, that if they will not turn, they will not enter into His rest; yet wicked they are, and wicked they will be, no matter what God and man will say to them. Carnal they are, and carnal they will be; worldly they are, and worldly they will be – even though God has told them that the love of the world is enmity to God (James 4:4), and that if anyone loves the world (in that measure), *the love of the Father is not in him* (1 John 2:15).

Consequently, these people are willing to be condemned, though not directly. They are willing to walk in the way to hell, and love the specific cause of their torment, although they do not want hell itself, and do not love the pain that they must endure.

Is not this the truth of your case? You do not want to burn in hell, but you will kindle the fire by your sins and will cast yourselves into it. You do not want to be tormented with demons forever, but you will do that which will certainly result in that despite all that can be said against it. It is just as if you would say, "I will drink this poison, yet I will not die"; "I will cast myself headlong from the top of a steeple, yet I will not kill myself"; "I will thrust this knife into my heart, but I will not take my life"; or "I will put this fire into the thatch of my house, yet I will not burn it."

This is how it is with wicked people. They want to be wicked, and they live after the flesh and the world, yet they do not want to be condemned. Do you not know, though, that the means lead to the end? Do you not know that God, by His righteous law, has concluded that you must repent or perish? He who intends to ingest poison may as well plainly say, "I intend to kill myself," for it will prove no better in the end, even if he might have loved it for the sweetness of the sugar that was mixed with it, and would not be persuaded that it was poison, but thought he could take it and still be alright. However, it is not his imagination and confidence that will save his life.

So if you want to be a drunkard, a fornicator, worldly, or live after the flesh, you may as well say plainly, "I intend to be condemned," for so you will be unless you turn. Would you not rebuke the foolishness of a murderer who would say, "I will kill, but I will not be hanged," when he knows that if he does the one, the judge in justice will assure that the other is done? If he says, "I intend to murder," he may as well plainly say, "I intend to be hanged," and if you intend to continue in a carnal life, you may as well plainly say, "I intend to go to hell."

2. Moreover, the wicked will not use those means without which there is no hope of their salvation. He who will not eat may as well plainly say that he will not live – unless he can tell how to live without food. He who will not go on his journey may as well plainly say that he will not come to the end of his journey. He who falls into the water and will not come out, nor allow anyone else to help him out, may as well plainly say that he wants to drown. Therefore, if you are carnal and ungodly and refuse to be converted or to use the means by which you could be converted, but think it is more bother than necessary, you may as well plainly say that you choose to be condemned – for if you have found a way to be saved without conversion, you have done that which was never done before.

3. This is not all, but the wicked are unwilling even to partake of salvation itself. Even though they may somewhat desire that which they call by the name of heaven, yet when heaven itself is considered in the true nature of the delight, they do not really desire it, but their hearts are quite against it. Heaven is a state of perfect holiness and of continual love and praise to God, and the wicked have no heart for this. They have no mind for the imperfect love, praise, and holiness that are to be attained here, much less for that which is so much greater. The joys of heaven are of so pure and spiritual a nature that the heart of the wicked cannot truly desire them.

> The joys of heaven are of so pure and spiritual a nature that the heart of the wicked cannot truly desire them.

By this time, you may see on what basis it is that God concludes that the wicked choose their own destruction. They will not turn, even though they must turn or die. They would rather risk certain misery than be converted, and then to quiet themselves in their sins, they will make themselves believe that they will nevertheless escape.

II. As this controversy or question is a matter of wonder in that people would be such enemies to themselves as to willingly cast away their souls, so are the disputants. It is a matter of wonder that God would stoop so low as to plead the case with us Himself, and also that people would be so strangely blind and obstinate as to need all this in so plain a case, and even to resist all this when their own salvation is at stake.

It is no wonder that they will not hear us who are men when they will not hear the Lord Himself. As God said when He sent the prophet to the Israelites, *The house of Israel will not hearken unto you; for they will not hearken unto me; for all the house of Israel are impudent and hardhearted* (Ezekiel 3:7). It is no wonder that they can argue against a godly minister or a godly neighbor when they will argue against the Lord Himself, even against the plainest passages of His Word, and think that they have reason on their side.

When they weary the Lord with their words, they say, *Wherein have we wearied him?* (Malachi 2:17). The priests who despised His name dare to ask, *Wherein have we despised thy name?* (Malachi 1:6). And when they pollute His altar and make the table of the Lord contemptible, they dare to ask, *Wherein have we polluted thee?* (Malachi 1:7). But the Lord says, *Woe unto him that striveth with his Maker! Let the potsherds strive with the potsherds of the earth: shall the clay say to him that fashioneth it, What makest thou?* (Isaiah 45:9).

Question: Why does God reason the case with man?

Answer: 1. Man is a creature of reason, and therefore is to be dealt with accordingly, and is to be persuaded and overcome by reason. God has provided them with reason that they might use it for Him. One would think that a reasonable creature would not go against the clearest and greatest reason in the world when it is set before him.

2. People will at least see that God required nothing of them that was unreasonable, but both in what He commands them, as well as what He forbids them, He has all the right reason in the world on His side. They have good reason to obey Him, but none to disobey Him. Therefore, even the condemned will be forced to justify God and confess that it was only reasonable that they should have turned to Him. They will be forced to condemn themselves and confess that they had little reason to cast themselves away by neglecting His grace in the day of their visitation.

Sinners, look up your best and strongest reasons if you intend to try to succeed in your way. You see now with whom you have to deal. What do you say, unconverted, carnal sinner? Do you dare try to dispute with God? Are you able to refute Him? Are you ready to argue with God? God asks you, "Why will you die?" Do you have a sufficient answer? Will you attempt to prove that God is mistaken and that you are in the right? Oh, what an undertaking that is!

Either He is mistaken or you are mistaken. He is for your conversion, and you are against it. He calls upon you to turn, and you will not. He urges you to do it now, even today, while it is called today (Hebrews 3:13), and you delay and think you will have enough time later. He says it must be a total change and that you must be holy and new creatures and born again, and you think it is enough to only do a little, that it is enough to patch up the old man without becoming new.

Who is in the right – God or you? God calls you to turn and to live a holy life, and you will not. By your disobedient life, it appears that you will not. If you say that you will, then why don't you? Why have you not done it all this time? Why have you not turned to Him yet? Your will has the command of your lives. We may certainly conclude that you are unwilling to turn when you do not turn. Why will you not? Can you give any reason for it that is worthy to be called a reason?

I am merely a worm, your fellow creature, of a shallow capacity, yet I dare challenge the wisest of you all to reason the case with me while I plead my Maker's cause – and I do not need to be discouraged when I know that I plead the cause that God pleads, and that I contend for Him who will have the best at last. If I only had these two general reasons against you, I am sure that you have no good reason on your side.

1. I am sure that any excuse or argument that is against the God of truth and reason is not a good argument. It cannot be light that is contrary to the sun. There is no knowledge in any creature except what it had from God, and therefore, no one can be wiser than God. It would be fatal presumption for the highest angel to try to compare himself with his Creator! What is it, then, for a lump of earth, an ignorant fool who does not know himself or his own soul, who knows only a little of the things that he sees, and who is more ignorant than many of his neighbors, to set himself against the wisdom of the Lord! It is one of the fullest discoveries of the horrible wickedness of carnal men, and the insanity of those who willingly sin, that such an absurd, blind creature dare contradict his Maker and call in question the Word of God. Yes, it is terrible that those people who are so ignorant that they cannot give us a reasonable answer concerning the very first principles of Christianity are yet so wise in their own conceit (Proverbs 26:12) that they dare question the plainest truths of God, and even contradict them and criticize them, when they can hardly speak sense

> I know that I plead the cause that God pleads, and that I contend for Him who will have the best at last.

and will believe them no further than what agrees with their foolish wisdom!

2. Just as I know that God is in the right, so I know that the case is so obvious and clear that the sinner pleads against that no one can have reason for it. Is it possible that anyone can have any reason to break his Maker's laws, any reason to dishonor the Lord of glory, and any reason to abuse the Lord who bought him? Is it possible that anyone can have any good reason to condemn his own immortal soul?

Observe the Lord's question: *Turn ye, turn ye . . . ; for why will ye die?* Is eternal death something to be desired? Are you in love with hell? What reason do you have to knowingly perish? If you think you have some reason to sin, should you not remember that death is the wages of sin (Romans 6:23), and then consider whether you have any reason to destroy yourselves, body and soul, forever? You should not only ask whether you love the adder, but also whether you love the sting. It is a strange thing for someone to cast away his everlasting happiness and to sin against God when no good reason can be given for it, but the more anyone argues for it, the more foolish he shows himself to be.

If you were offered a kingdom for every sin that you commit, it would not be good sense, but insanity to accept it. If by every sin you could obtain the highest thing on earth that the flesh desires, it would be of no considerable value to persuade you in reason to commit it. If it were to please your greatest or dearest friends, to obey the greatest ruler on earth, to save your life, or to escape the greatest earthly misery – all these are of no consideration to entice someone with good sense and reason to commit even one sin. If your right hand or right eye would hinder your salvation, it would be most beneficial for you to cast it away rather than to go to hell to save it, for there is no saving a part when you lose the whole (Matthew 5:29-30).

So exceedingly great are the matters of eternity that nothing in this world deserves even once to be named in comparison with them; nor can any earthly thing, even if it were life, or crowns, or kingdoms, be a reasonable excuse for neglecting matters of such high and everlasting consequence. A person can have no reason to resist his ultimate end. Heaven is such a thing that if you lose it, nothing can supply the lack or make up the loss; and hell is such a thing that if you suffer in hell, nothing can remove your misery or give you ease and comfort. Therefore, nothing can be a valuable consideration to excuse you for neglecting your own salvation, for our Savior says, *What shall it profit a man if he shall gain the whole world, and lose his own soul?* (Mark 8:36).

Oh, if you only knew what we are now speaking to you of, you would have other thoughts of these things. If the devil could come to the saints in heaven who live in the sight and love of God, and would offer them worldly pleasures, pleasant company, or sports to entice them away from God and glory, how do you think they would entertain the idea? If he would offer them to be kings on the earth, do you think this would entice them down from heaven? Oh, with what hatred and holy scorn they would reject the idea! And why would you not do so if you had heaven open to your faith and simply had faith to see it?

There is not a soul in hell who does not now know that it was a foolish exchange to let go of heaven for fleshly pleasure, and that it is not a little entertainment, pleasure, worldly riches, honor, or the good will or word of men that will quench the fires of hell or benefit him who loses his soul. Oh, if you had heard what I believe, if you had seen what I believe, and that on the certainty of the Word of God, you would say there can be no reason to justify anyone destroying his soul. You would not dare sleep quietly another night unless you had resolved to turn and live.

If you see someone put his hand in the fire until it burns off, you would marvel at it, but this is something that someone may have reason for, as Bishop Cranmer had when he burned off his hand for endorsing Roman Catholicism. If you see someone cut off a leg or an arm, it is a sad sight, but there may be a good reason for this also, as some people have had this done to save their lives. It is difficult to see someone give his body to be tormented with chains and torture, or to be burned to ashes, and refuse deliverance when it is offered, but a person may have good reason for this, as you may see in Hebrews 11:33-36, and as many hundreds of martyrs have recently done.

However, for someone to forsake the Lord who made him, and to run into the fire of hell when he is told of it and urged to turn that he may be saved – this is something that can have no reason in the world to justify or excuse it. Heaven will make up for the loss of anything that we can lose to obtain it, or for any labor that we expend for it, but nothing can pay for the loss of heaven.

I ask you now to let God's Word come nearer to your heart. Just as you are convinced that you have no reason to destroy yourselves, so tell me what reason you have to refuse to turn and live to God. What reason does the most excessive worldly person, drunkard, or ignorant, careless sinner have why he should not be as holy as anyone you know, and be as careful for his soul as anyone else? Will not hell be as intolerable to you as to others? Should not your own souls be as dear to you as theirs is to them? Does not God have just as much authority over you? Why, then, will you not become a sanctified person as well as they?

When God brings the matter down to the very principles of nature, and shows that you have no more reason to be ungodly than you have to destroy your own souls, if you will still not understand and turn, it seems that you are in a desperate situation.

Either you have good reason for what you do, or you do not. If not, will you go against reason itself? Will you do that for which you have no justification? If you think you have a good reason, produce it and make the best of your matter. Reason the case a little with me, your fellow creature. This is far easier to do than to reason the case with God. Tell me here before the Lord, as if you were to die this hour, why you will not resolve to turn this day, before you move from where you are. What reason do you have to deny or to delay? Do you have any reasons that satisfy your own conscience for it, or any that you dare acknowledge and plead at the judgment seat of God? If you have, let us hear them. Bring them forth, and make them good. But what poor stuff, what nonsense, instead of reasons, we daily hear from the ungodly! If it were not for the worth of their immortal souls, I would be ashamed to name them.

Objection 1: If no one will be saved except those whom you speak of who are converted and sanctified, heaven will be very empty. Then may God help a great many!

Answer: It seems that you think that God does not know, or else that He is not to be believed! Do not base everything upon the little that you know. God has thousands and millions of His sanctified ones, but they are few in comparison of the world, as Christ Himself has told us: *Enter ye in at the strait gate: for wide is the gate, and broad is the way, that leadeth to destruction, and many there be which go in thereat: because strait is the gate, and narrow is the way, which leadeth unto life, and few there be that find it* (Matthew 7:13-14). It better serves you to make that use of this truth that Christ teaches you. *And he went through the cities and villages, teaching, and journeying toward Jerusalem. Then said one unto him, Lord, are there few that be saved? And he said unto them, Strive to enter in at the strait gate: for many, I say unto you, will seek to enter in, and shall not be able* (Luke 13:22-24). Christ said to His sanctified ones, *Fear not, little flock, for it is your Father's good pleasure to give you the kingdom* (Luke 12:32).

Objection 2: I am sure that if people like me go to hell, I will have plenty of company.

Answer: Will that be any ease or comfort to you? Do you think you would not have enough company in heaven? Will you be destroyed because you want company? Will you not believe that God will execute His threatenings because there are so many who are guilty? These are all unreasonable thoughts.

Objection 3: All people are sinners, even the best of them.

Answer: Yes, but not all are unconverted sinners. The godly do not live in blatant sins, and their very shortcomings are their grief and burden, which they daily desire, pray, and strive to be rid of. Sin does not have dominion over them (Romans 6:14).

Objection 4: I do not see that those who profess to be Christians are any better than other people. They will overreach and oppress and are as covetous as anyone.

Answer: No matter how hypocrites are, it is not so with those who are sanctified. God has thousands and tens of thousands who are otherwise, even though the malicious world accuses them of what they can never prove, and of that which never entered into their hearts. The wicked commonly accuse them of sins of the heart, which no one can see except God, because they cannot accuse them of such wickedness in their lives as they are guilty of themselves.

Objection 5: But I am not an adulterer, drunkard, or oppressor, so why would you call upon me to be converted?

Answer: You were born after the flesh and have lived after the flesh as well as others! Is it not as great a sin as any of these for someone to have an earthly mind, to love the world above God, and to have an unbelieving, unhumbled heart? Let me tell you more. Many people who avoid disgraceful sins are as firmly glued to the world, are as much slaves to the flesh, are as unfamiliar with God, and are as contrary to heaven in their more respectable course as others are in their more shameful, notorious sins.

Objection 6: I do not intend anyone any harm, nor do I do any harm; why, then, would God condemn me?

Answer: Is it no harm to neglect the Lord who made you and the work for which you came into the world? Is it no harm to prefer the creature before the Creator and to neglect grace that is daily offered to you? It is the depth of your sinfulness to be so unaware of it. The dead do not feel that they are dead. If you were made alive, you would see more that is improper in yourself, and you would be amazed at yourself for downplaying it.

Objection 7: I think you want to make people crazy under pretense of converting them. It is enough to afflict the brains of simple people to think so much on matters too high for them.

Answer: 1. Can you be more unsound than you already are? At least, can there be a more dangerous form of insanity than to neglect your everlasting welfare and to knowingly destroy yourselves?

2. A person is never truly in his right mind until he is converted. He does not really know God, or sin, or Christ, or the world, or himself, or what his purpose is on earth so as to set himself about it – until he is converted. The Scriptures say that the wicked are unreasonable people (2 Thessalonians 3:2), and that the wisdom of the world *is foolishness with God* (1 Corinthians 3:19). It is said of the prodigal son that when he came to himself, he resolved to return (Luke 15:17). What a strange wisdom this is that people will disobey God and run toward hell out of fear that they will be considered fools!

> A person is never truly in his right mind until he is converted.

3. What is there in the work that Christ calls you to that would drive a person out of his senses? Is it loving God, calling upon Him, comfortably thinking of the glory to come, forsaking our sins, loving one another, and delighting ourselves in the service of God? Are these things that would make people lose their minds?

4. Because you say that these matters are too high for us, you accuse God Himself since He made this our work, gave us His Word, and commanded all who desire to be blessed to meditate on it day and night (Joshua 1:8). Are the matters that we are made for, and that we live for, too high for us to take part in? This is plainly to dehumanize us and to make beasts of us, as if we were like those who must engage in nothing higher than what belongs to flesh and earth. If heaven is too high for you to think about and consider, it will be too high for you to ever possess.

5. If God would sometimes allow any weak-headed person to be distracted by thinking about eternal things, this is because they misunderstand them and run without a guide. Of the two options, I would rather be in this situation than in that of the foolish, unconverted world that views their distraction as their wisdom.

Objection 8: I do not think that God cares so much about what people think, speak, or do as to make such a big deal about it.

Answer: It seems, then, you consider the Word of God to be false. Then what will you believe? Maybe you think that your own reason might teach you better if you do not believe the Scriptures. You can see that God regards us in such a way that He condescended to make us, and He still preserves us, daily upholds us, and provides for us. Will any wise person make a careful plan for nothing? Will you make or buy a clock or watch for daily use, and not care whether it keeps time well or not?

Certainly if you do not believe that the specific eye of Providence observes your hearts and lives, you cannot believe or expect any specific Providence to observe your needs and troubles, or to help you. If God had such little care for you as you imagine, you would never have lived until now. A hundred diseases would have endeavored to first destroy you. Yes, the demons would have visited you and would have taken you away alive, just as the large fish devour the smaller, and as ravenous beasts and birds devour others. You cannot think that God made man for no purpose or use, and if He made him for any, it was surely for Himself. Can you really think that He does not care whether His purpose is accomplished and whether we do the work that we are made for?

By this atheistic objection, you suppose that God made and upheld all the world in vain, for what are all other lower creatures for except for man? Why does the earth bear us and nourish us, and the beasts serve us with their labors and lives, and so of the rest? Has God made such a glorious habitation, placed mankind to live in it, and made all of creation for man – and does He look for nothing at his hands, nor care how he thinks, speaks, or lives? This is most unreasonable.

Objection 9: It was a better world when people did not make such a big deal about the Christian religion.

Answer: (1) It has always been the custom to praise the times past. That world that you speak of was inclined to say it was a better world in their forefather's days, and they said the same about their forefathers. This is just an old custom because we all feel the evil of our own times, but we do not see that which was before us.

(2) Maybe you speak as you think. Those who are of the world think the world is at its best when it is agreeable to their minds and when they have the most fun and worldly pleasure. I do not doubt that the devil, as well as you, would say that it was a better world then, for then he had more service and less disturbance. The truth, though, is that the world is at its best when God is most loved, regarded, and obeyed. How else will you know when the world is good or bad except by this?

Objection 10: There are so many ways and religions that we do not know which one to be part of, and therefore we will remain even as we are.

Answer: Because there are many, will you be of that way that you may be sure is wrong? None are further out of the way than worldly, carnal, unconverted sinners, for not only do they err in this or that opinion, as many religious groups do, but the very scope and direction of their lives is wrong. If you were going on a journey that your life depended on, would you stop or turn aside because you came to an intersection, or because you saw some travelers go one way and some another way, some climb over a fence, and some miss the way completely? Would you not rather be even more careful to inquire of and follow the right way? If you have some employees who do not know how to do the work properly, and some who are unfaithful, would you be pleased with any of the rest who would therefore be lazy and not work well for you because they see their companions work so poorly?

Objection 11: I do not see that life goes any better with those who are so godly than with other people. They are as poor and have as much trouble as others.

Answer: Yes, and maybe they have even more trouble when God finds it appropriate. They do not take earthly prosperity for their wages. They have laid up their treasure and hopes in another world, or else they are not truly Christians. The less they have, the more awaits them, and they are content to wait until then.

Objection 12: When you have said all that you can, I am resolved to hope positively, trust in God, do as well as I can, and not make such a fuss about it.

Answer: (1) Are you doing as well as you can when you will not turn to God, but your heart is against His holy and diligent service? It is truly as well as you want, but that is your affliction.

(2) My desire is that you would hope and trust in God, but what is it that you hope for? Is it to be saved if you turn and are sanctified? You have God's promise for this, and therefore I tell you to fully hope for it. However, if you hope to be saved without conversion and a holy life, this is not to hope in God, but it is hoping in Satan or yourselves, for God has given you no such promise. In fact, He has told you the contrary. It is Satan and self-love that made you such promises and raised you to such hopes.

If you hope to be saved without conversion, this is not to hope in God, but it is hoping in yourselves, for God has given you no such promise.

Well, if these and similar objections are all you have to say against conversion and a holy life, your all is nothing, and worse than nothing. If these and similar reasons seem sufficient to convince you to forsake God and cast yourselves into hell, we must ask the Lord to deliver you from such reasons, from such blind understandings, and from such senseless, hardened hearts.

Do you dare to stand and affirm one of these reasons at the judgment seat of God? It will not help to say then, "Lord, I did not turn because I had so much to do in the world," or "because I did not like the lives of some who professed to be Christian," or "because I saw people of so many beliefs!" Oh, how easily the light of that day will confound and shame such reasonings as these! Did you have the world to look after? Then let the world that you served now pay you your wages and save you if it can. Did you not have a better world to look after first? Were you not commanded to seek first God's kingdom and righteousness, and were you not promised that other things would be added to you if you did (Matthew 6:33)?

Were you not told that *godliness is profitable unto all things, having the promise of the life that now is, and of that which is to come* (1 Timothy 4:8)? Did the sins of professing Christians hinder you? Instead, you should have been even more cautious and should have learned by their falls to beware. You should have been more careful rather than more careless. It was the Bible, and not their lives, that was your standard.

Did the many opinions of the world hinder you? Your standard, the Holy Scriptures, only taught you one way, and that was the right way. If you had followed that, even in as much as was plain and easy, you would never have gone wrong.

Will not such answers as these confound and silence you? If these will not, God has others that will. When He asked the man, *Friend, how camest thou in hither not having a wedding garment?* (Matthew 22:12) – that is, what are you doing in My church among professed Christians without a holy heart and life – what answer did He make? The text says that *he was speechless.* He had nothing to say. The clearness of the case and the majesty of God will then easily stop the mouths of the most confident of you, even though you will not be silenced by anything we can say to you now, but will defend your cause no matter how bad it is. I already know that there is no excuse or reason that you can give me now that will do you any good at last, when your case must be opened before the Lord and before all the world.

I hardly think that your own consciences are very satisfied with your reasons. If they are, then it seems that you have not as much as an intent to repent. But if you do intend to repent, it seems you do not put much confidence in the reasons that you bring against it.

What do you say, unconverted sinners? Do you have any good reasons to give why you should not turn, and immediately turn, with all your hearts? Will you go to hell in spite of reason itself? Consider what you do in time, for it will soon be too late for you to consider. Can you find any fault with God, or with His work or wages? Is He a bad master? Is the devil, whom you serve, a better master? Is the flesh a better master? Is there any harm in a holy life? Is a life of worldliness and ungodliness better? Do you think in your consciences that it would do you any harm to be converted and live a holy life? What harm can it do to you? Would it harm you to have the Spirit of Christ within you and to have a cleansed, purified heart?

If it is bad to be holy, why does God say, *Be ye holy, for I am holy* (1 Peter 1:15-16; Leviticus 20:7)? Is it evil to be like God? Is it not said that God made man in His own image (Genesis 1:27)? This holiness is His image. Adam lost this, and Christ by His Word and Spirit wants to restore this to you, as He does to all whom He will save. How is it that people are baptized into the Holy Spirit as their Sanctifier, and yet you will not be sanctified by Him, but think it is an affliction for you to be sanctified?

Tell me truly, as before the Lord, even though you are reluctant to live a holy life, would you not rather die in the case of those who do so than of others? If you were to die this day, would you not rather die in the case of a converted person than of an unconverted? Would you not rather die as a holy and heavenly person than of a carnal, earthly person? Would you not say as Balaam, *Let me die the death of the righteous, and let my last end be like his!* (Numbers 23:10)? Why, then, will you not now be of the mind that you will be part of then? Now or later, you must come to this – either to be converted, or to wish you had been when it is too late.

The friends you lose when you are converted would have only enticed you to hell, but could not have delivered you.

What is it that you are afraid of losing if you turn? Is it your friends? You will simply change friends. God will be your friend, and Christ and the Spirit will be your friends. Every Christian will be your friend. You will get one Friend who will be of more advantage to you than all the friends in the world. The friends you lose would have only enticed you to hell, but could not have delivered you. However, the Friend you get will save you from hell and will bring you to His own eternal rest.

Is it your pleasures that you are afraid of losing? You think you will never have a joyous day again once you are converted. How sad that you would think it is a greater pleasure to live in foolish sports and entertainment, and to please your flesh, than to live in the believing thoughts of glory, in the love of God, and in righteousness, peace, and joy in the Holy Spirit, in which the state of grace consists (Romans 14:17)!

If it would be a greater pleasure for you to think of your lands and inheritance, if you were lord of all the country, than it is for a child to play, then why would it not be a greater joy to you to think of the kingdom of heaven being yours than to think of all the riches or pleasures of the world? As it is only simple childishness that makes children so delight in toys that they would not leave them for all your lands, so it is but simple worldliness, carnality, and wickedness that makes you so much delight in your houses and lands, meat and drink, and ease and honor that you would not part with them for the heavenly delights.

What will you do for pleasure when these are gone? Do you not think of that? When your pleasures end in horror and go out like a candle, the pleasures of the saints are then the highest. I have had only a little taste of the heavenly pleasures in the foresight of the blessed approaching day, and in the present views of the love of God in Christ, but I have also taken too deep of a drink of earthly pleasures – so that you may see that if I am partial, it is on your side. Yet I must profess, from that little experience, that there is no comparison. There is more joy to be had in one day, if the sun of life shines clear upon us, in the state of holiness, than in a whole life of sinful pleasures.

A day in His courts is better than a thousand anywhere else.

I had rather be a doorkeeper in the house of God than to dwell in the tents of wickedness (Psalm 84:10). The joy of the wicked is like the laughter of a crazy person who does not know his own misery. This is why Solomon says of such laughter, *it is mad; and of mirth, what doeth it?* (Ecclesiastes 2:2).

> *It is better to go to the house of mourning than to go to the house of feasting; for that is the end of all men, and the living will lay it to his heart. Sorrow is better than laughter; for by the sadness of the countenance the heart is made better. The heart of the wise is in the house of mourning; but the heart of fools is in the house of mirth. It is better to bear the rebuke of the wise than to hear the song of fools; for as the crackling of thorns under a pot, so is the laughter of the fool.* (Ecclesiastes 7:2-6)

Your loudest laughter is only like that of someone who is tickled; he laughs when he has no cause of joy. Judge whether this is a wise man's part. It is only your carnal, unsanctified nature that makes a holy life seem disagreeable to you and a path of worldliness seem more delightful. If you will only turn, the Holy Spirit will give you another nature and inclination, and then it will be more pleasant to you to be rid of your sin than it is now to keep it. You will then say that you did not know what a comfortable life was until now, and that it was never well with you until God and holiness were your delight.

Question: Why are people so unreasonable in the matter of salvation? They have sense enough in other matters. What makes them so reluctant to be converted that so many words are needed in such a plain case, and even that is usually rejected, as most people will live and die unconverted?

Answer: To name them only in a few words, the causes are these:

1. People are naturally in love with the earth and flesh. They are born sinners, and their nature has an enmity to God and godliness, just as the nature of a serpent has to a man. When all that we can say goes against the habitual inclination of their natures, it is no wonder that it prevails so little.

2. They are in darkness, and they do not know the very things they hear. They are like a man who was born blind and hears high praise of the light; but what will hearing do unless he sees it? They do not know who God is, or what the power of the cross of Christ is, or who the Spirit of holiness is, or what it is to live in love by faith. They do not know the certainty, suitableness, and excellency of the heavenly inheritance. They do not know what conversion and a holy mind and conversation are, even when they hear of them. They are in a fog of ignorance. They are lost and bewildered in sin, like a man who has lost himself in the night and does not know where he is, nor knows how to find his way until the daylight comes again.

> People are naturally in love with the earth and flesh.

3. They are purposely confident that they do not need to be converted, but only need some partial change. They believe that they are on the way to heaven already and are already converted – when they are not. It is difficult to show someone that he is not on the way to heaven if he is wrongly convinced that he is on the way to heaven.

4. They have become slaves to their flesh, and they are immersed in the world to make provision for it. Their lusts, passions, and appetites have distracted them, and have such power over them that they cannot tell how

to deny them or how to care about anything else. The drunkard says, "I love a glass of alcohol, and I cannot abstain." The glutton says, "I love good food, and I cannot refrain." The fornicator says, "I love to have my lust fulfilled, and I cannot refuse it." The gambler loves to have his sports, and he cannot stop. They have even become captivated slaves to their flesh, and their very persistence has become a weakness. What they do not want to do, they say they cannot. The worldly person is so obsessed with earthly things that he has neither heart, mind, nor time for heavenly things. Instead, just as the lean cows ate up the fat ones in Pharaoh's dream (Genesis 41:4), so this lean and barren earth eats up all the thoughts of heaven.

5. Some people are so carried away by the stream of evil company that they are possessed with harsh thoughts of a godly life by hearing them speak against it; or at least they think they may attempt to do as they see most people do, so they continue in their sinful ways. When one person is cut off and cast into hell, and another is taken away from among them to the same condemnation, it does not alarm them much because they do not see where they have gone. Poor reprobates, they continue in their ungodliness despite all this, for they little know that their companions are now agonizing in torment. In Luke 16, the rich man in hell would gladly have had someone warn his five brothers so that they would not end up in that place of torment. It is likely that he knew their minds and lives, knew that they were hurrying there, and they did not think that he was there – and they would not have believed anyone who would have told them so.

I remember a story that a gentleman told me he saw upon Acham Bridge over the Severn River. A man was driving a flock of fat lambs, and something met them and hindered their passage. One of the lambs leaped upon the wall of the bridge. Its legs slipped, and it fell into the stream. The rest of the sheep saw that, and one after another, they leaped over the bridge into the stream until all or almost all were drowned. Those that were behind did not know what had become of those that had gone before, but thought they might try to follow their companions. However, as soon as they were over the wall and were falling headlong, their situation was altered. This is how it is with unconverted, carnal people. Someone near them dies and drops into hell, and another follows the same way, yet they will follow them because they do not think about where they are going. Once the hour of death has opened their eyes, though, and they see what is on the other side of the wall, even in another world, what then would they give to be where they once were!

6. In addition, they have a scheming, malicious enemy whom they do not see. He plays his game in the dark, and it is his main business to prevent their conversion. Therefore, he desires to keep them where they are by persuading them not to believe the Scriptures, or not to trouble their minds with these matters, or by persuading them to think negatively of a godly life. The Enemy tries to convince them that more is required than is necessary and that they may be saved without conversion and without all this bother. Satan tries to convince them that God is so merciful that He will not condemn them – or at least that they may continue a little longer, enjoy their pleasure, and follow the world a little longer still, and then let it go and repent later. By

> Satan tries to convince them that God is so merciful that He will not condemn them.

such deceptive, misleading lies as these, the devil keeps most people in his captivity and leads them to his misery.

These and similar hindrances keep many thousands of people unconverted, when God has done so much, and Christ has suffered so much, and godly ministers have said so much for their conversion. When their reasons are silenced and they are not able to answer the Lord who calls after them, *Turn ye, turn ye . . . ; for why will ye die?* – the majority of people still reject God. There is nothing more we can do after all this except to sit down and lament their voluntary misery.

I have now shown you the reasonableness of God's commands and the unreasonableness of wicked people's disobedience. If nothing will serve to persuade them, but people will still refuse to turn, we are next to consider who is in fault if they are damned. This brings me to the last principle.

Principle 7

If the wicked will not turn after all this, it is not God's fault that they perish, but it is their own fault. Their own stubbornness and rebellion is the cause of their damnation. Therefore, they die because they choose to die. They refuse to turn.

If you choose to go to hell, what remedy is there? God here acquits Himself of your blood. It will not lie on Him if you are lost. A negligent minister may face some blame, and those who encourage you in sin or do not hinder you in sin may bear some responsibility, but you can be certain that none of the fault can be placed upon God. Concerning His unprofitable vineyard, the Lord says, *Judge, I pray you, betwixt me and my vineyard. What could have been done more to my vineyard that I have not done in it?* (Isaiah 5:1-4). When He had planted it in productive soil, fenced it, gathered out the stones, and planted it with the best vines, what more could He have done?

He has made you men and women, and has blessed you with reason. He has provided you with all external necessities. All creatures are at your service. He has given you a righteous, perfect law. When you had broken it and ruined yourselves, He had compassion on you and sent His Son by a miracle of condescending mercy to die for you and to be a sacrifice for your sins, and He was in Christ reconciling the world to Himself (2 Corinthians 5:19)!

The Lord Jesus has made you a covenant of a gift of Himself, and eternal life with Him, on the condition that you will simply accept it and turn. Based upon this reasonable condition, He has offered you the free pardon of all your sins! He has written this in His Word, has sealed it by His Spirit, and has sent it by His faithful ministers. They have made the offer to you hundreds of times and have called you to accept it and to turn to God. In His name, they have appealed to you, they have reasoned the case with you, and they have answered all your frivolous objections.

God has long waited for you. He has even patiently allowed you to abuse Him to His face! He has mercifully sustained you in the midst of your sins. He has compassed you about with all sorts of mercies. He has also mixed in afflictions to remind you of your foolishness and to call you to your senses. His Spirit has often been striving with your hearts, saying, "Turn, sinner, turn to Him who is calling you. Where are you going? What are you doing? Do you know what the end will be for you? How long will you hate your friends and love your enemies? When will you let go of it all and turn and deliver yourself up to God, giving your Redeemer the possession of your soul? When will you turn?"

These pleadings have been used with you, and when you have delayed, you have been urged to hurry. God has called to you, *Today if ye will hear his voice, harden not your hearts* (Hebrews 3:15). Why not listen now without any more delay?

Life has been set before you. The joys of heaven have been opened to you in the gospel. Their certainty has been demonstrated. The certainty of the everlasting torments of the damned has been declared to you. Unless you would have seen heaven and hell, what more could you want?

Christ has been, as it were, set forth crucified before your eyes (Galatians 3:1). You have been told a hundred times that you are only lost people until you come to Him. Just as often, you have been told of the evil of sin; of the vanity of sin, the world, and all the pleasures and wealth it can provide; of the shortness and uncertainty of your lives; and of the endless duration of the joy or torment of the life to come. All this, and more than this, you have been told, and told again, even until you were tired of hearing it and until you could begin to disregard it because you had heard it so often – like the blacksmith's dog, that because of familiarity is brought to sleep under the noise of the hammers and as the sparks fly around his ears. Even though all this has not converted you, you are still alive and could have mercy to this day if you simply had a heart to contemplate it. Let reason itself now be the judge whether it is God's fault or your own if after all this you remain unconverted and will be condemned. If you die now, it is because you choose to die.

> Let reason itself now be the judge whether it is God's fault or your own if you remain unconverted.

What more should be said to you, or what course should be taken that is more likely to prevail? Are you able to truly say, "We would gladly have been converted and become new creatures, but we could not. We would gladly have forsaken our sins, but we could not. We would have changed our company, our thoughts, and our conversation, but we could not"?

Why could you not if you really desired to? What kept you from doing so except the wickedness of your hearts? Who forced you to sin, or who held you back from duty? Have you not had the same teaching, time, and liberty to be godly as your godly neighbors had? Then why could you not have been godly as well as they? Were the church doors shut against you, or did you not keep yourselves away, or sit and sleep, or hear as if you did not hear?

Did God put any exceptions in His Word against you when He invited sinners to turn from sin and turn to Him, and when He promised mercy to those who do turn? Did He say, "I will pardon all who repent except you?" Did He shut you out from the liberty of His holy worship? Did He forbid you to pray to Him any more than others? You know He did not. God did not drive you away from Him, but you forsook Him and ran away yourselves. When He called you to Him, you would not come.

If God had left you out of the general promise and offer of mercy, or had said to you, "Get away. I want nothing to do with people like you. Do not pray to me, for I will not hear you. No matter how much you repent and cry for mercy, I will not listen to you," – if God had left you nothing to trust to but desperation, then you might have a fair excuse. You might have said, "Why should I repent and turn when it will do no good?" But this was not your case.

You could have had Christ to be your Lord and Savior, your Head and Husband, but you would not because you did not feel that you were sick enough for the Physician, and because you did not want to get rid of your disease. In your hearts, you said as those rebels did, *We will not have this man to reign over us* (Luke 19:14). Christ would have gathered you under the wings of His salvation, but you did not want Him to (Matthew 23:37). What desires for your good the Lord expressed in His holy Word! With what compassion He stood over you and said, *Oh that my people had hearkened unto me, and that they had walked in my ways!* (Psalm 81:13). *O that there were such an heart in them, that they would fear me, and keep all my commandments always, that it might be well with them and with their children forever!* (Deuteronomy 5:29). *O that they were wise, that they understood this, that they would consider their latter end!* (Deuteronomy 32:29).

He would have been your God, and would have done all for you that your souls could well desire, but you loved the world and your flesh above Him, and therefore you would not listen to Him. Although you sang His praises and gave Him high titles, yet when it came to turning from self and sin and surrendering all to Him, you wanted nothing to do with Him. It is no wonder, then, if He gave you up to your own heart's lust, and you walked in your own counsel (Psalm 81:11-12).

God lowers Himself to reason with you and plead the case with you, and He says to you:

What is there in Me, or in My service, that you are so much against Me? What harm have I done to you, sinner? Have I deserved this unkind dealing at your hand? I have shown you many mercies; for which of them do you despise Me? Is it I, or is it Satan who is your enemy? Is it I, or is it your carnal self that would destroy you? Is it a holy life, or is it a life of sin that you have cause to run from? If you are ruined, you did it to yourself by forsaking Me, the Lord who would have saved you [Jeremiah 2:17].

Does not your own wickedness correct you, and your sin admonish you? You can see that it is an evil and bitter thing that you have forsaken Me [Jeremiah 2:19]. What iniquity have you found in Me that you have followed after vanity and have forsaken Me [Jeremiah 2:5-6]? He calls out, as it were, to the beasts, to hear the quarrel He has against you. *Hear ye, O mountains, the Lord's controversy, and ye strong foundations of the earth; for the Lord hath a controversy with his people, and he will plead with Israel. O my people, what have I done unto you, and wherein have I wearied you? Testify against me, for I brought thee up out of Egypt, and redeemed thee* [Micah 6:2-4].

Hear, O heavens, and give ear, O earth, for the Lord hath spoken. I have nourished and brought up children, and they have rebelled against me. The ox knoweth his owner, and the ass his master's crib; but Israel doth not know, my people doth not consider! Ah, sinful nation, a people laden with iniquity, a seed of evildoers [Isaiah 1:2-4]. *Do you thus requite the* LORD, *O foolish people and unwise? Is not he thy Father that bought you? Hath he not made thee, and established thee?* [Deuteronomy 32:6].

When He saw that you forsook Him, even for nothing, and turned away from the Lord of life to hunt after the chaff and emptiness of the world, He told you of your foolishness and called you to a more profitable use of your life:

Wherefore do you spend money for that which is not bread, and your labor for that which satisfieth not? Hearken diligently unto me, and eat ye that which is good, and let your soul delight itself in fatness. Incline your ear, and come unto me; hear, and your soul shall live; and I will make an everlasting covenant with you, even the sure mercies of David. . . . Seek ye the LORD*ord while he may be found, call ye upon him while he is near. Let the wicked forsake his way, and the unrighteous man his thoughts, and let him return unto the* LORD, *and he will have mercy upon him; and to our God, for he will abundantly pardon.* (Isaiah 55:2-3, 6-7; see also Isaiah 1:16-18)

When you would not hear, what complaints you have caused Him to bring against you, placing the blame on you because of your defiance and stubbornness! *Be astonished, O heavens, at this, and be horribly afraid, be ye very desolate, saith the* LORD. *For my people have committed two evils; they have forsaken me, the fountain of living waters, and hewed them out cisterns, broken cisterns, that can hold no water* (Jeremiah 2:12-13).

Christ has often proclaimed that free invitation to you: *Let him that is athirst come, and whosoever will, let him take the water of life freely* (Revelation 22:17). However, you caused Him to complain, after all His offers: *Ye will not come to me, that ye might have life* (John 5:40).

He has invited you to feast with Him in the kingdom of His grace, and you have had excuses based upon your property, your possessions, and your worldly business. When you would not come, you have said you could not, and you moved Him to resolve that you would never taste of His supper (Luke 14:16-25). Whose fault is it now but your own? What can you say is the main cause of your damnation but your own will? You choose to be condemned. The entire case is expressed in the Bible itself:

> When you would not come to Christ's feast, you moved Him to resolve that you would never taste of His supper.

> *Wisdom crieth without; she uttereth her voice in the streets; she crieth in the chief place of concourse, in the openings of the gates: in the city she uttereth her words, saying, How long, ye simple ones, will ye love simplicity, and the scorners delight in their scorning, and fools hate knowledge? Turn ye at my reproof. Behold, I will pour out my Spirit upon you, I will make known my words unto you. Because I have called, and ye refused; I have stretched out my hands, and no man regarded; but ye have set at naught all my counsel, and would none of my reproof. I also will laugh at your calamity; I will mock when your fear cometh; when your fear cometh as desolation, and your destruction cometh*

as a whirlwind; when distress and anguish cometh upon you, then shall they call upon me, but I will not answer; they shall seek me early, but they shall not find me, for that they hated knowledge, and did not choose the fear of the LORD.

They would none of my counsel; they despised all my reproof; therefore shall they eat of the fruit of their own way, and be filled with their own devices. For the turning away of the simple shall slay them, and the prosperity of fools shall destroy them. But whoso hearkeneth unto me shall dwell safely, and shall be quiet from fear of evil. (Proverbs 1:20-33)

I thought it best to recite the whole text to you because it so fully shows the reason for the destruction of the wicked. It is not because God would not teach them, but because they would not learn. It is not because God would not call them, but because they would not turn at His reproof. Their self-will is their downfall.

From what has been said, you may further learn the following things:

1. Not only can you see what blasphemy and impiety it is to try to place the blame of people's destruction upon God, but you can also see how unfit these wicked wretches are to bring such an accusation against their Maker! They cry out against God, saying that He gives them no grace, that His threatenings are severe, and that it is unreasonable that all who are not converted and sanctified should be condemned. They think it is a harsh standard that a short sin would have endless suffering. They say that if they are condemned, they cannot help it, even though in the meantime, they are bringing about their

own destruction, even the destruction of their own souls, and will not be persuaded to stop their destructive ways. They think that God would be cruel to condemn them, yet they are so cruel to themselves that they will run into the fire of hell when God has told them that it is only a little way ahead of them, and neither pleadings nor threatenings, nor anything that can be said, will stop them.

We see them almost destroyed. Their careless, worldly, carnal lives tell us that they are in the power of the devil. We know that if they die before they are converted, all the world cannot save them. Knowing the uncertainty of their lives, we are afraid every day that they might drop into the fire, and therefore we plead with them to care about their own souls and not to destroy themselves when mercy is at hand, but they will not hear us. We plead with them to cast away their sin and come to Christ without delay, and to have some mercy on themselves, but they refuse it all; yet they think that God must be cruel if He condemns them.

> You are told that if you choose to keep your sins, you must keep the curse of God with them, yet you want to keep them.

Oh, rebellious, miserable sinners! God is not cruel to you, but you are cruel to yourselves. You are told that you must turn or burn, yet you refuse to turn. You are told that if you choose to keep your sins, you must keep the curse of God with them, yet you want to keep them. You are told that there is no way to happiness except by holiness, yet you will not be holy.

What more do you want God to say to you? What would you have Him do with His mercy? He offers it to you, and you refuse it. You are in the ditch of sin and misery, and He offers you His hand to help you out, but you refuse His help. He wants to cleanse you of your sins, and you would rather keep them. You love your lust, gluttony, sports, and drunkenness, and you will not let them go. Would you have Him bring you to heaven whether you want to go or not? Would you have Him bring you and your sins to heaven together?

That is an impossibility. You may as well expect Him to turn the sun into darkness. Will an unsanctified, carnal heart be in heaven? No! It cannot be! Nothing unclean can enter into it (Revelation 21:27). *What communion hath light with darkness? And what concord hath Christ with Belial?* (2 Corinthians 6:14-15). God says, *All day long I have stretched forth my hands unto a disobedient and gainsaying people* (Romans 10:21).

What will you do now? Will you cry to God for mercy? God calls upon you to have mercy upon yourselves, and you will not! Ministers see the poisoned cup in the drunkard's hand. They tell him there is poison in the cup, and they desire him to have mercy on his soul and abstain from alcohol, but he refuses to listen! He must drink it, and he will. He loves it, and therefore, even though hell comes next, he says he cannot help it. What should one say to such people as these?

We tell the ungodly, careless, worldly person that such a life will not help them or ever bring them to heaven. If a lion were behind you, you would start walking faster. However, when the curse of God is at your back, and Satan and hell are at your back, will you not get moving? Instead, you ask, "What need is there of all this fuss?"

Is an immortal soul of no more worth? Oh, have mercy upon yourselves! But they will have no mercy on themselves, nor pay any attention to us. We tell them that their end will be bitter (2 Samuel 2:26). Who can dwell with everlasting fire (Isaiah 33:14)? Yet they will have no mercy on themselves. These shameless transgressors will still say that God is more merciful than to condemn them, when they are the ones cruelly and unmercifully running upon condemnation. If we would go to them and beg them, we cannot stop them. If we would fall on our knees and plead with them, we cannot stop them, but they will go to hell – yet they refuse to believe that they are going there.

If, for the sake of God who made them and preserves them, for the sake of Christ who died for them, and for the sake of their own souls, we plead with them to care about their own souls and to go no further in the way to hell, but to come to Christ while His arms are open, to enter into the state of life while the door stands open, and to receive His mercy while it may be had, they will not be persuaded. Even if we would die for it, we cannot as much as get them to occasionally consider the matter and turn; yet they still say, "I hope God will be merciful."

Have you never considered what He said in Isaiah 27:11? *It is a people of no understanding; therefore he that made them will not have mercy on them, and he that formed them will show them no favor.* If another person will not clothe you when you are naked, or feed you when you are hungry, you will say he is unmerciful. If he would cast you into prison, or beat and torment you, you would say he is unmerciful. Yet you will do a thousand times more against yourselves, even casting away both soul and body forever, and never complain of your own unmercifulness!

Yes, and you consider God, who waited upon you all this time in His mercy, to be unmerciful if He punishes you after all this. Unless the holy God of heaven will allow these ungodly people to trample upon His Son's blood, and with the Jews, as it were, to spit again in His face and do *despite unto the Spirit of grace* (Hebrews 10:29); and joke about sin; and ridicule holiness; and place more importance upon their fleshly pleasures than upon God's saving mercy; and unless, after all this, He will save them by the mercy that they cast away and wanted nothing to do with, God Himself will be called unmerciful by them! However, He will be justified when He judges, and He will not stand or fall at the judgment seat of a sinful worm.

I know there are many specific objections and complaints that are brought by them against the Lord, but I will not try to answer them specifically here, as I have already done so in my *Treatise of Judgment*,[3] to which I will refer them. If the disputing part of the world had been as careful to avoid sin and destruction as they have been busy in searching after their cause and indirectly attributing them to God, they could have exercised their minds more profitably, could have wronged God less, and could have better helped themselves.

When such an ugly monster as sin is within us, when such a heavy thing as punishment is on us, and when such a dreadful thing as hell is before us, one would think it would be an easy question who is in the wrong – whether God or man is the main or blameworthy cause. Some people are such favorable judges of themselves that they are more inclined to accuse infinite perfection and goodness itself than their own hearts. They imitate their first parents, who said, "The serpent tempted me," and "The woman whom You gave to me gave me the fruit, and I did eat" – secretly implying that God was the cause.

In the same way, these people say, "The understanding that You gave to me was unable to discern. The will that You gave to me was unable to make a better choice. The objects that You set before me enticed me. The temptations that You allowed to attack me prevailed against me." Some people are so afraid to think that God can make a self-determining creature that they dare not deny Him that which they take to be His prerogative – to be the determiner of the will in every sin, as the first effective and immediate physical cause. Many people could be content to stop blaming God for causing so much evil if they could only reconcile it with His being the main cause of good – as if truths would no longer be truths if we are unable to see them in their perfect order and coherence. Because our

---

3   The title of the book is *Two Treatises: The first of Death, on 1 Cor. 15:26. The Second of Judgment, on 2 Cor. 5:10, 11*, first printed in London in 1672.

tangled minds cannot perceive them properly together, nor assign each truth its proper place, we presume to conclude that some must be cast away. This is the fruit of proud self-conceit, when men and women do not receive God's truth as children in holy submission to the omniscience of our Teacher, but as critics who are too wise to learn.

Objection: But we cannot convert ourselves until God converts us. We can do nothing without His grace. *It is not of him that willeth, nor of him that runneth, but of God that showeth mercy* (Romans 9:16).

Answer: God has two decrees of mercy to show: first He shows the mercy of conversion, and then He shows the mercy of salvation. He will give the latter only to those who desire and who run, and He has promised it only to them. The former is to make them willing who are unwilling. Although your own willingness and efforts do not deserve His grace, your willful refusal deserves that it should be denied to you. Your shortcoming is your very unwillingness itself, which does not excuse your sin, but makes it greater. You could turn if you were simply truly willing. If your wills themselves are so corrupted that nothing except effectual grace will move them, you have even more cause to seek for that grace, to yield to it, and to do what you can in the use of means rather than neglecting it and setting yourselves against it. Do what you are able to do first, and then complain about God for denying you grace if you still have reason to do so.

Objection: But you seem to suggest all this time that man has free will.

Answer: 1. The dispute about free will is beyond your ability. Therefore, I will not burden you with anything more now than this. Your will is naturally a free capability, or a self-determining ability. However, it is viciously inclined, and hesitant to do good. We see, therefore, by sad experience, that it does not have a virtuous moral freedom, but it is this wickedness of it that deserves the punishment. I appeal to you not to deceive yourselves with opinions. Let the case be your own. If you had an enemy who was so malicious as to attack you and beat you, or take away the lives of your children, would you excuse him because he said he did not have free will, but it was his nature, and he cannot choose unless God gives him grace? If you had an employee who robbed you, would you accept such an answer from him? Could not every thief and murderer who is to be hanged after a trial give such an answer? They could say, "I do not have free will. I cannot change my own heart. What can I do without God's grace?" Will they therefore be acquitted? If not, why then would you think to be acquitted for a path of sin against the Lord?

2. Therefore, you may also observe these three things together: (1) what a shrewd tempter Satan is, (2) what a deceitful thing sin is, and (3) what a foolish, corrupted creature man is. Satan is indeed a shrewd tempter, for he persuades the majority of the world to go into everlasting fire when they have so many warnings and other attempts to dissuade them as they have! Sin is indeed a deceitful thing, for it beguiles so many thousands of people to part with everlasting life for something so low and completely unworthy! Man is indeed a foolish creature, for he will be defrauded of his salvation for nothing, and even for something that is known to be nothing, and to be defrauded by an enemy, and a known enemy.

You would think it would be impossible for anyone in his senses to be persuaded for a pittance to cast himself into the fire, or water, or into a coal pit, to the destruction of his life – yet people will be enticed to cast themselves into hell. If your natural lives were in your own hand, that you would not die until you would kill yourselves, how long would most of you live? Yet when everlasting life is so much in your own hands, under God, that you cannot be destroyed until you destroy yourselves, how few of you will refrain from your own destruction! What a foolish thing man is, and what a beguiling and deceptive thing sin is!

3. You may learn from this that it is no great wonder if wicked people hinder others on the way to heaven, that they want as many unconverted people as they can, that they would entice them into sin, and that they try to keep them in it. Can you expect them to have mercy on others when they will have none upon themselves? Can you expect them to hesitate much at the destruction of others when they do not hesitate to destroy themselves? They do no worse by others than they do by themselves.

4. Lastly, you may learn from this that the greatest enemy to man is himself. The greatest judgment in this life that can happen to him is to be left to himself. The great work that grace has to do is to save us from ourselves. The greatest accusations and complaints of people should be against themselves, and the greatest work we have to do ourselves is to resist ourselves. The greatest enemy that we should daily pray against, watch against, and strive against is our own carnal hearts and wills. The greatest part of your work, if you want to do good to others and help them to heaven, is to save them from themselves – even from their own blind understandings, corrupted wills, perverse affections, destructive passions, and unruly senses. I only name all these for brevity's sake, and will leave them to your further consideration.

Well, now that we have discovered the great offender and murderer of souls (even ourselves, our own wills), what is left for you to do except to judge according to the evidence? Therefore, confess this great iniquity before the Lord, be humbled for it, and do so no more.

I will add a few more words to further convince you, to humble you, and to reform you, if there is still any hope.

1. We know so much about the exceedingly gracious nature of God, who is willing to do good and who delights to show mercy, that we have no reason to suspect Him of being the culpable cause of our death, or to call Him cruel. He made everything good, and He preserves and maintains it all. The eyes of all wait upon Him, and He gives them their meat in due season. He opens His hand and satisfies the desires *of every living thing* (Psalm 145:15-16). Not only is He *righteous in all His ways* (and therefore will deal justly) and *holy in all His works* (and therefore is not the author of sin), but He is also good to all, and His tender mercies are over all His works (Psalm 145:17-19).

As for humans, we know that their minds are dark, their wills perverse, and their affections carry them so recklessly that they are equipped by their foolishness and corruption to such a work as destroying themselves. If you saw a lamb that had been killed in the field, would you first suspect a sheep or a wolf to have killed the sheep if they were both standing near? If you see a house broken open, and the people murdered, would you first suspect the prince or judge, who is wise and just and had no need, or would you suspect a known thief or murderer? I say, therefore, as James said, *Let no man say when he is tempted, I am tempted of God, for God cannot be tempted with evil, neither tempteth he any man [to try to get him to sin], but every man is tempted when he is drawn away of his own lust and enticed. Then when lust hath conceived, it bringeth forth sin; and sin, when it is finished, bringeth forth death* (James 1:13-15).

114

You see here that sin is the offspring of your own sinful desire, and God is not to be accused of it. Death is the offspring of your own sin, and it is the fruit that it will produce as soon as it is ripe. You have a supply of evil in yourselves, as a spider has of poison, from where you are bringing forth harm to yourselves and spinning such webs that entangle your own souls. Your nature shows that you are the cause.

2. It is evident that you are your own destroyers, for you are quite ready to consider almost any temptation that is offered to you. Satan is hardly more ready to move you to any evil than you are ready to hear and to do as he wants you to do. If he tries to tempt your understanding to error and animosity, you yield. If he wants to hinder you from good resolutions, it is soon done. If he desires to quiet any good desires or affections, it is soon done. If he wants to kindle any lust, vile affections, or sinful desires in you, it is soon done. If he tries to have you think evil thoughts, speak sinful words, or commit unholy deeds, you are so free and willing that he does not need to push you to do so. If he attempts to keep you from holy thoughts, words, and ways, he can merely suggest it, and you gladly comply. You do not examine his suggestions, resist them with any determination, throw them out as he casts them in, nor quench the sparks that he attempts to kindle – but you side with him, meet him halfway, embrace his suggestions, and tempt him to tempt you. It is easy for him to catch such greedy fish that are looking for bait and will take the bare hook.

> Sin is the offspring of your own sinful desire, and God is not to be accused of it.

3. Your destruction is evidently of yourselves, in that you resist all who try to help save you and want to do you good, or prevent you from ruining yourselves. God wants to help and save

you by His Word, and you resist it; it is too strict for you. He wants to sanctify you by His Spirit, and you resist and quench Him. If anyone reproves you for your sin, you reply in anger with evil words. If he tries to lead you to a holy life and tell you of your present danger, you give him little thanks, but either tell him to mind his own business because he will not have to answer for you, or you brush him aside with heartless thanks and will not turn when you are urged to do so.

If godly ministers want to privately instruct and help you, you will not go to them. Your unhumbled souls do not feel much need of their help. If they try to teach you, you think you are too old to be taught, even though you are not too old to be ignorant and unholy. No matter what they say to you for your good, you are so self-conceited and wise in your own eyes, even in the depth of ignorance, that you will not consider anything that does not agree with your present conceits, but you will contradict your teachers, as if you were wiser than they. By your ignorance, disobedience, foolish arguments, wayward evasions, and ungrateful rejections, you resist all that they can say to you so that no good that is offered to you can find any welcome, acceptance, or consideration with you.

> Your destruction is evidently of yourselves, in that you resist all who try to help save you.

4. Moreover, it is apparent that you are destroying yourself in that you infer the matter of your sin and destruction even from the blessed God Himself. You do not like the ways of His wisdom. You do not like His justice, but take it for cruelty. You do not like His holiness, but you want to think that He is similar to you (Psalm 50:21) and that He downplays sin as you do. You do not like His truth, but would like to have His threatenings, even His uncompromising threatenings, proven to be false. His goodness, which you seem most highly to approve, you partly resist because it would lead

you to repentance, and you partly abuse, to the strengthening of your sin, as if doing so allows you to sin more freely because God is merciful and because His grace so much abounds.

5. Yes, you even bring down destruction from the blessed Redeemer, and you bring down death from the Lord of life Himself! Nothing more emboldens you in sin than that Christ has died for you, as if now the danger of death were over and you can boldly risk your soul. You live as if Christ has become a servant to Satan and your sins and must serve you while you are offending Him. Because He is the Physician of souls and is able to save to the uttermost all who come to God by Him (Hebrews 7:25), you think He must allow you to refuse His help and throw away His cures, and that He must save you whether you will come to God by Him or not. Therefore, a great part of your sins are brought about by your bold presumption upon the death of Christ, not considering that He came to redeem His people from their sins (Matthew 1:21), to sanctify them a special people to Himself (Titus 2:14), and to conform them in holiness to the image of their heavenly Father and to their Head (1 Peter 1:15-16; Colossians 3:10; Philippians 3:9-10).

6. You also bring down your own destruction from all the providences and works of God. When you think of His eternal foreknowledge and decrees, it is to harden you in your sin, or to possess your minds with argumentative thoughts, as if His decrees might spare you the labor of repentance and a holy life, or else were the cause of your sin and death. If He afflicts you, you complain. If He causes you to prosper, you forget Him even more and consider even less the life that is to come. If the wicked prosper, you forget the end that will set all accounts straight, and you are ready to think it is just as good to be wicked as godly. Thus you bring about your death from all of this.

7. You misuse to your ruin all the creatures and mercies of God to you. He gives them to you as the tokens of His love and furnishings for His service, and you turn them against Him to the pleasing of your flesh. You eat and drink to please your appetite, and not for the glory of God and to enable you to perform His work (1 Corinthians 10:31). Your clothes become a source of pride to you. Your riches take your heart away from heaven. Your honors and commendations puff you up. If you have health and strength, it makes you more secure and you forget your end. Yes, and even other people's mercies are perverted by you to your harm. If you see their honors and dignity, you are moved to envy them. If you see their riches, you are ready to covet them. If you look upon beauty, you are stirred up to lust. It is good if godliness itself is not a disgrace to you.

8. The very gifts that God bestows on you, and the ordinances of grace that He has instituted for His church, you turn to sin. If you have better abilities than others, you grow proud and self-conceited. If you have only ordinary gifts, you consider them to be special grace. You take the simple hearing of your duty for so good a work as if it would excuse you for not obeying it. Your prayers are turned into sin because you regard iniquity in your hearts (Psalm 66:18), and you do not depart from iniquity when you call on the name of the Lord (2 Timothy 2:19). Your prayers are abominable because you turn away your ear from hearing the law (Proverbs 28:9), and you are more ready to offer the sacrifice of fools, thinking that you do God some special service, than to hear His Word and obey it (Ecclesiastes 5:1).

9. The people with whom you speak, and all their actions, you make the occasions of your sin and destruction. If they live in the fear of God, you hate them. If they live ungodly, you imitate them. If the wicked are many, you think you may more boldly

follow them. If the godly are few, you are more encouraged to despise them. If they walk strictly, you think they are too precise. If one of them falls in a particular temptation, you stumble and turn away from holiness because others are imperfectly holy, as if you were justified in breaking your neck because some other people have, by their carelessness, sprained a muscle or broken a bone. If a hypocrite discloses himself, you say, "They are all alike," and you think that you are as honest as the best. A professing Christian can hardly make any mistake, but because he cuts his finger, you think you may boldly cut your throat.

If godly ministers deal plainly with you, you say they scold. If they speak gently or coldly, you either sleep under them, or are little more affected than the seats you sit upon. If any errors creep into the church, some gladly consider them, and others reproach the Christian doctrine for them, which is mostly against them. If we would try to bring you away from any ancient rooted error, which can plead only two or three or seven hundred years' custom, you are as much offended with a motion for reformation as if you were to lose your life by it, and you cling to old errors while you speak out against new ones.

Hardly a difference can arise among the ministers of the gospel but you will bring about your own death from it. You will not hear, or at least not obey, the unquestionable doctrine of any of those who do not agree with your delusions. One person will not hear a minister because he reads his sermons. Another person will not hear him because he does not read them. One will not hear him because he says the Lord's Prayer, and another will not hear him because he does not use it. One person will not hear those who are for formal church ceremonies, and another will not hear those who are against it. It is clear that the ungodly

> It is clear that the ungodly are self-destroyers, and that their damnation is of themselves.

are self-destroyers, and that their damnation is of themselves. I could show you many other cases in which you turn all that comes near you to your own destruction.

Upon the consideration of what has been said, and upon reviewing your own ways, I think you should consider what you have done, and you should be ashamed and deeply humbled to remember it. If you are not, I ask you to consider these following truths:

1. To destroy yourself is to sin against the deepest principle in your natures – the principle of self-preservation. Everything naturally desires or inclines to its own happiness, welfare, or perfection, and will you bring about your own destruction? When you are commanded to love your neighbors as yourselves, it is supposed that you naturally love yourselves; but if you love your neighbors no better than you now love yourselves, in that you bring about your own damnation, it seems you want all the world to be damned.

2. How completely you obstruct your own intentions! I know you do not intend your own damnation, even when you are obtaining it. You think you are only doing good to yourselves by gratifying the desires of your flesh, but sadly, it is only as a drink of cold water in the midst of a burning fever, or as the scratching of a severe rash, which increases the disease and pain. If you indeed want to have pleasure, profit, or honor, seek them where they are to be found, and do not hunt after them in the way to hell.

3. What a pity it is that you would do against yourselves that which no one else on earth or in hell can do! If all the world were combined against you, or all the demons in hell were combined against you, they could not destroy you without yourselves, nor make you sin except by your

own consent – and will you do against yourselves that which no one else can do? You have hateful thoughts of the devil because he is your enemy and seeks your destruction, and will you be worse to yourselves than the devil will be? If you had a heart to understand it, you would see that this is how it is with you. When you run into sin, when you run from godliness, and when you refuse to turn at the call of God, you do more against your own souls than people or demons could do. If you would rack your brain to try to do the greatest harm to yourself, you could not devise anything greater.

4. You are false to the trust that God has committed to you. He has much entrusted you with your own salvation, and will you betray your trust? He has set you, with all diligence, to keep your hearts (Proverbs 4:23), and is this how you keep them?

5. You even forbid all others to show compassion to you when you will have no compassion on yourselves. If you cry out to God in the day of your calamity for mercy, what can you expect Him to do except to push you away and say, "No. You would not have mercy on yourself. What brought this upon you but your own obstinance?" If your brethren see you in everlasting misery, how will they feel sorry for you when you destroyed yourself and would not be dissuaded?

6. It will everlastingly make you your own tormentor in hell to think that you brought yourselves willingly to that misery. Oh, what a painful thought it will be to forever know that this was your own doing! You were warned of this day, and warned again, but you would not listen. You willfully sinned and willfully turned away from God! You had time as well as others, but you misused it.

You had teachers as well as others, but you refused their instruction. You had holy examples, but you did not imitate them. You were offered Christ and grace and glory as well as others, but you had more concern for your fleshly pleasures! You had a price in your hands, but you did not have the heart to get wisdom (Proverbs 17:16). Can it fail to torment you to think of your present foolishness?

Oh, that your eyes were open to see what you have done in willingly wronging your own souls! Oh, that you better understood these words of God:

> *Hear instruction and be wise, and refuse it not. Blessed is the man that heareth me, watching daily at my gates, waiting at the posts of my doors. For whoso findeth me findeth life, and shall obtain favor of the LORD. But he that sinneth against me wrongeth his own soul. All they that hate me love death.* (Proverbs 8:33-36)

Conclusion

Now I am come to the conclusion of this work. My heart is troubled to think how I will leave you. I fear that even after all this, the flesh will still deceive you, the world and the devil will keep you asleep, and I will leave you as I found you – until you awake in hell. Although I write this in care of your poor souls, I am afraid of this as I know the obstinacy of a carnal heart. However, I can say with the prophet Jeremiah that the Lord knows I have not desired this *woeful day* (Jeremiah 17:16). I have not, with James and John, desired that fire might *come down from heaven* to consume those who refuse Jesus Christ (Luke 9:54).

Rather, all this time I have been trying to prevent you from spending your eternity in the eternal fire. I wish this had not been necessary. I wish that God and your conscience might have been as willing to spare me this labor as some of you could have been. Dear friends, I am so unwilling for you to lie in everlasting fire and to be shut out of heaven, if it is possible to prevent it, that I will ask you once more what you now resolve to do. Will you turn, or will you die?

I look upon you as a physician looks upon his patient who has a dangerous disease and who says to him, "Although the disease is far advanced, simply take this medicine and abstain from these few things that are harmful to you, and you will live; but if you will not do this, you will die." What would you think of such a person if the physician, and all the friends he has, cannot persuade him to take one medicine to save his life, or to give up one or two poisonous things that would kill him?

This is your situation. No matter how far you are gone in sin, simply now turn, come to Christ, and take His remedies – and your soul will live. Give up your deadly sins by repentance, and do not return to the poisonous vomit anymore, and you will do well. If we only had to deal with your body, we might partly know what to do for you. Although you would not consent, you could still be held down or bound while the medicine was poured down your throat, and hurtful things could be kept from you.

You may be condemned against your will because you sinned with your will, but you cannot be saved against your will.

However, this cannot be done in regard to your soul. We cannot convert you against your will. We cannot carry madmen to heaven in chains. You may be condemned against your will because you sinned with your will, but you cannot be saved against your will. The wisdom of God has thought proper to place people's salvation or destruction exceedingly much upon the choice of their own will so that no one will go to heaven who did not choose the way to heaven, and no one will go to hell who will not be obligated to say, "I have what I chose. My own will brought me here." If I could only get you to be willing, to be thoroughly, resolvedly, and habitually willing, the work would be more than half done. Must we lose our friends, and must they lose their God, their happiness, and their souls for lack of this? God forbid! It is a strange thing to me that people are so unnatural and foolish in the greatest matters who in lesser things are civil and courteous and good neighbors.

For all I know, I have the love of all, or almost all, of my neighbors, so that if I would send to any person in the town, parish, or county, and make a reasonable request of them, they would grant it to me; yet when I come to request of them the greatest matter in the world, for themselves and not for me, many of them give me nothing but a patient hearing. I do not know whether people think a man in the pulpit is very sincere or not, and that he means what he says, for I think I have many neighbors who would believe me and consider what I say if I were sitting familiarly with them and telling them what I have seen and done or known in the world; but when I tell them from the infallible Word of God what they themselves will see and know in the world to come, they show by their lives that they either do not believe it or do not much consider it. If I met any of them on the way and told them that there is a coal pit over there, or there is quicksand, or there are thieves lying in wait for them, I could persuade them to turn aside, but when I tell them that Satan lies in wait for them, that sin is poison to them, and that hell is not a matter to be joked about, they go on as if they did not hear me. Truly, neighbors, I am as sincere with you in the pulpit as I am in any friendly conversation, and if you will ever pay attention to what I say, please let it be here.

I do not think there is one person here who would not be willing to save my soul if it were in your power to do so – although I cannot promise that you would leave your sins for it. Tell me, you drunkard, are you so cruel to me that you would not go without a few glasses of alcohol if you knew it would save my soul from hell? Would you rather have me burn there forever than for you to live soberly as other people do? If so, may I not say that you are an unmerciful monster and not a man?

If I came hungry or naked to one of your doors, would you not part with more than a glass of alcohol to help me? I am confident you would. If it were to save my life, I know that some of you would risk your own lives, and yet will you not be prevailed upon to part with your worldly pleasures for your own salvation? Would you give up a hundred glasses of alcohol to save my life, if it were in your power, and will you not do it to save your own soul?

I profess to you that I am as fervently begging with you today for the saving of your own souls as I would be for my own needs if I were forced to come begging to your doors. Therefore, if you would hear me then, hear me now. If you would show compassion to me then, be convinced now to have compassion on yourselves. I do again plead with you, as if it were on my bended knees, that you would listen to your Redeemer – and turn that you may live.

All you who have lived in ignorance, carelessness, and presumption to this day; all you who have been drowned in the cares of the world and have no concern regarding God and eternal glory; all you who are enslaved to your fleshly desires of food and alcohol, sports and lusts; all you who do not know the necessity of holiness and were never acquainted with the sanctifying work of the Holy Spirit upon your souls; all you who have never embraced your blessed Redeemer with a living faith and with admiring and thankful appreciation of His love; and you who have never felt a greater appreciation for God and heaven, and a warmer love to them than to your fleshly prosperity and the things below – I earnestly plead with you, not only for my sake, but for the Lord's sake and for your soul's sake, that you do not go on one more day in your former condition, but look around you and cry to God for converting grace so that you may be made new creatures and may escape the torment that is just a little before you.

If you will ever do anything for me, grant me this request: turn from your evil ways and live. Deny me anything that I will ever ask you for myself if you will only grant me this. If you deny me this, I do not care for anything else that you would give me.

If you would ever do anything at the request of the Lord who made you and redeemed you, do not deny Him this, for if you deny Him this, He cares for nothing else that you will give Him. If you would ever have Him hear your prayers, grant your requests, and help you at the hour of death and on the day of judgment, or in any of your crises, do not deny His request now in the day of your prosperity. Believe that death and judgment and heaven and hell are other matters when you get near to them than they seem to be to carnal eyes a long distance away. If you believed this, you would hear such a message as I bring you now with a more awakened, reverent heart.

Although I cannot hope so well of all people, I will hope that some of you by this time are intending to turn and live. I hope that some of you are ready to ask me what the Jews asked Peter when *they were pricked in their hearts* and said, *Men and brethren, what shall we do?* (Acts 2:37). You might say, "How may we come to be truly converted? We are willing, if we would only know our duty. God forbid that we should choose destruction by refusing conversion, as we have done until now."

If these are the thoughts and intents of your hearts, I say of you as God did of a promising people, *They have well said all that they have spoken. O that there was such a heart in them, that they would fear me, and keep all my commandments always!* (Deuteronomy 5:28-29). Your intents are good. Oh, that there were simply a heart in you to perform these purposes! In the hope of this, I will gladly give you direction as to what to do, and will do so briefly so that you may more easily remember it and do it.

Direction 1: If you desire to be converted and saved, strive to understand the necessity and true nature of conversion – for what, from what, to what, and by what it is that you must turn.

Consider what a regrettable condition you are in until the hour of your conversion so that you may see that it is not a condition you should be content in. You are under the guilt of all the sins that you ever committed, and you are under the wrath of God and the curse of His law. You are bondslaves to the devil, and you are daily employed in his work against the Lord, yourselves, and others. You are spiritually dead and distorted, as being destitute of the holy life, nature, and likeness of the Lord. You are unfit for any holy work, and you do nothing that is truly pleasing to God. You are without any promise or assurance of His protection, and you live in continual danger of His justice, not knowing what hour you may be taken away to hell. You are most certain to be damned if you die in that condition, and nothing short of conversion can prevent it. No matter what civilities or virtues you have, and no matter what changes you make, you are short of true conversion, and these things will never procure the saving of your soul. Keep the true sense of this natural misery, and also of the necessity of conversion, on your heart.

You must understand what it is to be converted: it is to have a new heart and nature, and a new way of life.

1. Consider **for what** you must turn. You must turn for the following reasons, and you may attain each objective. (1) You will immediately be made living members of Christ. You will have an interest in Him, you will be renewed after the image of God, and you will be adorned with all His graces. You will be made alive with a new and heavenly life. You will be saved from the tyranny of Satan and the dominion of sin, you will be justified from the curse of the law, and you will have forgiveness of all the sins of

your entire life. You will be accepted by God, you will be made His child, and you will have liberty with boldness to call Him Father. You can go to Him in prayer with all your needs, with a promise of acceptance. You will have the Holy Spirit to dwell in you, to sanctify you, and to guide you. You will have part in the brotherhood, communion, and prayers of the saints. You will be equipped for God's service. You will be freed from the dominion of sin. You will be useful and a blessing to the place where you live. You will have the promise of this life and of that which is to come. You will lack nothing that is truly good for you, and you will be enabled to bear your necessary afflictions. You may have some taste of communion with God in the Spirit, especially in all holy ordinances, where God prepares a feast for your souls. You will be an heir of heaven while you live on earth, and you may foresee by faith the everlasting glory – and so you may live and die in peace. No matter how low you are, your happiness will be incomparably greater than your misery.

How precious is every one of these blessings, which I only briefly mention, and which in this life you may receive!

(2) At death, your soul will go to Christ, and at the day of judgment, both soul and body will be justified and glorified and will enter into your Master's joy, where your happiness will consist in these specific details:

a. You will be perfected yourselves. Your mortal body will be made immortal, and the corruptible will put on incorruption (1 Corinthians 15:53). You will no more be hungry, thirsty, weary, or sick, nor will you need to fear shame, sorrow, death, or hell. Your soul will be perfectly freed from sin and perfectly suited for the knowledge, love, and praises of the Lord.

b. Your work will be to behold your glorified Redeemer, with all your holy fellow citizens of heaven, to see the glory of the most blessed God, to love Him perfectly, to be beloved by Him, and to praise Him everlastingly.

c. Your glory will contribute to the glory of the new Jerusalem, the city of the living God, which is more than to have a private blessing to yourselves.

d. Your glory will contribute to glorifying your Redeemer, who will everlastingly be magnified and pleased in you who are *the travail of his soul* (Isaiah 53:11), and this is more than glorifying yourself.

e. The eternal Majesty, the living God, will be glorified in your glory as He is magnified by your praises, as He communicates His glory and goodness to you, and as He is pleased in you and in His Son, as well as in the accomplishment of His glorious work in the glory of the new Jerusalem.

Even the poorest beggar among you who is converted will certainly and endlessly enjoy all this.

2. You must understand **from what** you must turn. In a word, you must turn from your carnal self. Pleasing the carnal self is the goal of all who are unconverted. You must turn from the flesh that wants to be pleased instead of God, even though it still entices you. You must turn from the world, which is the bait, and from the devil, who fishes for souls and is the deceiver. You must turn from all known and intentional sins.

3. You must know **to what** you must turn. You must turn to God as your goal, to Christ as the way to the Father, to holiness as the way appointed for you by Christ, and

to the use of all the helps and means of grace provided to you by the Lord.

4. Lastly, you must know **by what** you must turn. You must turn by Christ as the only Redeemer and Intercessor, by the Holy Spirit as the Sanctifier, by the Word as His instrument or means, and by faith and repentance as the means and duties on your part to be performed. All of this is of necessity.

Direction 2: If you want to be converted and saved, then be much in private, serious contemplation. Lack of this type of serious thought and contemplation troubles the world. Withdraw yourselves often into isolated seclusion, and there reflect upon the reason why you were made, of the life you have lived, of the time you have lost, and of the sins you have committed. Meditate upon the love, sufferings, and fulness of Christ. Think much about the danger you are in, of the nearness of death and judgment, of the certainty and excellency of the joys of heaven, of the certainty and terror of the torments of hell, and of the eternity of both. Contemplate the necessity of conversion and a holy life. Occupy your hearts in such considerations as these.

> Just as God will lighten the world by the sun so He will save people by His ministers, who are the lights of the world.

Direction 3: If you want to be converted and saved, read and heed the Word of God, which is the ordinary means. Read the Scripture, or hear it read, and other holy writings that apply it. Constantly attend the public preaching of the Word from godly men. Just as God will lighten the world by the sun, and not by Himself without it, so He will convert and save people by His ministers, who are the lights of the world (Matthew 5:14; Acts 26:17-18).

After God had miraculously humbled Paul, He sent Ananias to him (Acts 9:10-11), and when He had sent an angel to Cornelius, it was simply to tell him to send for Peter, who must tell him what to believe and do (Acts 10).

Direction 4: Give yourselves to God in a course of earnest, constant prayer. Confess and lament your former life, and beg Him for His grace to illuminate and convert you. Earnestly ask Him to forgive what is past, to give you His Spirit, to change your heart and life, to lead you in His ways, and to save you from temptation. Pursue this work daily, and do not be weary of it.

Direction 5: Immediately give up your known and willful sins. Take a stand, and go that way no longer. Be drunk no more, but avoid the very occasion of it. Cast away your lusts and sinful pleasures with abhorrence. Curse and swear and blaspheme no more. If you have wronged anyone, make restoration, as Zacchaeus did (Luke 19:8). If you will continue to commit your old sins, what blessing can you expect on the means for conversion?

Direction 6: If possible, immediately change your company if it is bad company – not by forsaking your necessary relations, but by leaving your unnecessary sinful companions. Instead, join yourselves with those who fear the Lord, and ask them about the way to heaven (Psalm 15:4; Acts 9:26).

Direction 7: Deliver yourselves up to the Lord Jesus as the Physician of your souls so that He may pardon you by His blood and sanctify you by His Spirit, and by His Word and ministers – the instruments of the Spirit. He is the way, the truth, and the life. No one can come to the Father except by Him (John 14:6). Nor is there any other name under heaven by which you can be saved (Acts 4:12). Study, therefore, His person and nature. Study what He has done for you, what He is to you, what He will be, and how He is ready and able to fully supply all your necessities.

Direction 8: If you truly intend to turn and live, do it quickly and without delay. If you are not willing to turn today, you are not willing to do it at all. Remember that all this time you are in your sins, under the guilt of many thousand transgressions, and under God's wrath. You stand at the very brink of hell. There is only a step between you and death (1 Samuel 20:3). This is not a condition for anyone in his right mind to be quiet in. Rise up quickly, then, and run for your lives, just as you would run out of your house if it were on fire.

Oh, if you only knew in what continual danger you live, what daily unspeakable loss you sustain, and what a safer and sweeter life you could live, you would not remain unconcerned, but you would quickly turn. Multitudes fail who deliberately delay when they are convinced that it must be done. Your lives are short and uncertain. What a sad situation you are in if you die before you fully turn! You have stayed away too long already, and you have wronged God too long. Sin gains strength while you delay. Your conversion will grow increasingly difficult and doubtful. You have much to do. Therefore, do not put it all off to the end for fear that God may forsake you and give you up to yourselves, for then you will be ruined forever.

> If you only knew in what continual danger you live, and what a sweeter life you could live, you would quickly turn.

Direction 9: If you will turn and live, do so sincerely, completely, and fully. Do not think that you can negotiate with Christ and divide your heart between Him and the world, that you can part with some sins and keep the rest, and that you can let go only of that which your flesh can spare. This is only deceiving yourself. In resolve and in heart, you must forsake all that you have, or else you cannot be His disciples (Luke 14:26, 33). If you will not take God and heaven for your portion; if you will not lay everything in this life at the feet of Christ, but you want to hold on to your good things here and have an earthly portion; if God and glory are not enough for you, then it is in vain to dream of salvation on these terms, for it will not be. No matter how religious you seem to be, if it is only a worldly righteousness, and if the flesh's prosperity, pleasure, or safety are still exceptions in your devotedness to God, this is as certain a way to death as open atheism, even though it is more convincing.

Direction 10: If you will turn and live, do it determinedly, and do not stand still and deliberate as if it were a doubtful case. Do not stand around wavering as if you were uncertain whether God or the flesh is the better master, whether sin or holiness is the better way, or whether heaven or hell is the better result. Away with your former lusts, and immediately, unceasingly, and wholeheartedly resolve! Do not be of one mind one day and of another mind the next, but be done with the world, and resolvedly give up yourselves and all that you have to God. Now – while you are reading or hearing this, resolve; before you sleep another night, resolve; before you move from this place, decide! Before Satan has time to distract you or entice you to change your mind, take a stand for God! You will never truly turn until you resolve, and do so with a firm, unchangeable decision.

Now I have done my part in this work so that you may turn at the call of God and live. What will become of it, I cannot tell. I have cast the seed at God's command, but it is not in my power to give the increase. I can go no further with my message. I cannot take it to your heart, nor can I make it work. I cannot do your part for you, which is to receive it and consider it. Nor can I do God's part by opening your heart to cause you to contemplate it. I cannot show heaven or hell to your sight, nor give you new and tender hearts. If I knew what more I could do for your conversion, I hope I would do it.

Closing Prayer

O You who are the gracious Father of spirits, You have declared that You do not delight in the death of the wicked, but rather that they turn and live. Do not deny Your blessing to these persuasive arguments and directions, and do not allow Your enemies to triumph in Your sight. Let not the great deceiver of souls prevail against Your Son, Your Spirit, and Your Word!

Have mercy on these poor unconverted sinners who have no hearts to have compassion on themselves or help themselves! Command the blind to see, the deaf to hear, and the dead to live, and do not let sin and death be able to resist You. Awaken the secure, resolve the unresolved, and strengthen the wavering. Let the eyes of sinners who read these lines be next engaged in weeping over their sins. Bring them to themselves and to Your Son before their sins have brought them to eternal hell. If You only say the word, these poor efforts will prosper to the winning of many souls to their everlasting joy and Your everlasting glory. Amen.

Richard Baxter - A Brief Biography

Richard Baxter, in his own words, preached "as a dying man to dying men." He lived a life of sincerity, devotion, and faithfulness to God. He is best known for his pastoral ministry in Kidderminster, England, and for his writings such as *The Reformed Pastor, A Call to the Unconverted, The Life and Death of the Reverend Joseph Alleine*, and *The Saints' Everlasting Rest*.

Baxter was born on November 12, 1615, in Rowton, England. He did not have a university education, but by diligent private study, he was ordained to the ministry at the age of twenty-three. He began preaching in Kidderminster, where he continued for the next nineteen years. During that time, from 1642–1647, Richard Baxter was also a chaplain in the parliamentary army. He was sick and in poor health during much of his life. Like the biblical prophets, he was sometimes seen as too outspoken, but this came from his love for God and opposition to the sin around him. He was a leading Nonconformist pastor, and was much respected for his godliness and for his pastoral dedication and ability.

Richard Baxter was not a supporter of the Anglican Church's episcopacy, so when he was offered the position of bishop of Hereford in 1660, he turned it down. As a result, he was not permitted to hold any position in the Anglican Church, he was not allowed to return to his position at Kidderminster, and he was not even allowed to preach.

On September 10, 1662, Richard Baxter married Margaret Charleton, who died in 1681. They had no children. However, Baxter deeply cared about families, even writing works such as *The Special Duties of Children Towards Their Parents*, *The Duties of Parents for Their Children*, and *The Special Duties of Children and Youth Towards God*.

Baxter faced much persecution during his life. His devotion was to God rather than to men or even to a church system, so people often opposed him from many different sides. He was imprisoned on several occasions for "crimes" such as meeting together with other Christians or for preaching without a license. For example, he spent a week in jail in 1669, and then, near the age of seventy, he was imprisoned for about a year and a half.

He is perhaps best known for his ministry at Kidderminster and for *The Reformed Pastor*. When Baxter arrived at Kidderminster, he stated that there was only about "one family in a street that worshipped God and called on His name." By the end of his ministry there, Baxter said, "On the Lord's days there was no disorder to be seen in the streets, but you might hear a hundred families singing psalms and repeating sermons as you passed through the streets. . . . There were some streets where there was not more than one family in the side of a street that did not so."

George Whitefield visited Kidderminster in 1743 and said that he was "greatly refreshed to find what a sweet savor of good Mr. Baxter's doctrine, works, and discipline remained to this day."

Richard Baxter lived what he taught, and he taught what he believed. One of his main points of emphasis in *The Reformed Pastor* was his belief that pastors should regularly visit the people of their parishes—their neighborhoods—to get to know their needs, especially spiritual. He did not promote mere social visits, but desired to help each member of the family know and follow Christ Jesus. Baxter himself visited about fourteen families every week, desiring to visit each of the eight hundred families in Kidderminster every year.

Richard Baxter died on December 8, 1691, at the age of seventy-six. A statue of Baxter still stands in Kidderminster to honor the life and ministry of this man of God.

Other Similar Titles

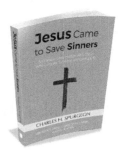

Jesus Came to Save Sinners, by Charles H. Spurgeon

This is a heart-level conversation with you, the reader. Every excuse, reason, and roadblock for not coming to Christ is examined and duly dealt with. If you think you may be too bad, or if perhaps you really are bad and you sin either openly or behind closed doors, you will discover that life in Christ is for you too. You can reject the message of salvation by faith, or you can choose to live a life of sin after professing faith in Christ, but you cannot change the truth as it is, either for yourself or for others. As such, it behooves you and your family to embrace truth, claim it for your own, and be genuinely set free for now and eternity. Come and embrace this free gift of God, and live a victorious life for Him.

Available where books are sold.

The Way to God, by Dwight L. Moody

There is life in Christ. Rich, joyous, wonderful life. It is true that the Lord disciplines those whom He loves and that we are often tempted by the world and our enemy, the devil. But if we know how to go beyond that temptation to cling to the cross of Jesus Christ and keep our eyes on our Lord, our reward both here on earth and in heaven will be 100 times better than what this world has to offer.

This book is thorough. It brings to life the love of God, examines the state of the unsaved individual's soul, and analyzes what took place on the cross for our sins. *The Way to God* takes an honest look at our need to repent and follow Jesus, and gives hope for unending, joyous eternity in heaven.

Available where books are sold.

Made in United States
Orlando, FL
04 July 2023

34753211R00095